Becoming a Project Leader

Alexander Laufer • Terry Little
Jeffrey Russell • Bruce Maas

Becoming a Project Leader

Blending Planning, Agility, Resilience, and Collaboration to Deliver Successful Projects

palgrave
macmillan

Alexander Laufer
University of Wisconsin-Madison,
Madison, Wisconsin, USA

Technion – Israel Institute of Technology
Haifa, Israel

Jeffrey Russell
Division of Continuing Studies
University of Wisconsin-Madison
Madison, Wisconsin, USA

Terry Little
Defense Systems Management College
Fairfax Station, Virginia, USA

Bruce Maas
School of Information
University of Wisconsin-Madison
Madison, Wisconsin, USA

ISBN 978-3-319-66723-2   ISBN 978-3-319-66724-9   (eBook)
https://doi.org/10.1007/978-3-319-66724-9

Library of Congress Control Number: 2017955386

Printed on acid-free paper

This Palgrave Macmillan imprint is published by Springer Nature
The registered company is Springer International Publishing AG
The registered company address is: Gewerbestrasse 11, 6330 Cham, Switzerland

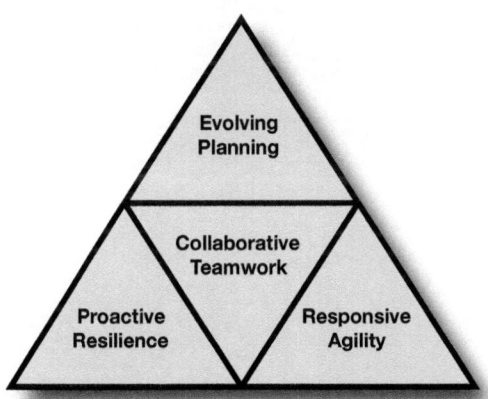

Foreword

I am biased. I want to write a foreword that will prompt you to read this book. I feel that it is a good bias, for worthy reasons, but it is a bias nonetheless. You see I consider our world a project world. The great challenges and world problems of our age—whether health care, security, education, space travel, economics—are approached through project management. You can be fashionable and call it another thing, but we solve our great challenges by using methods for bringing together people from various disciplines and committing to excellence in performance, speed, and cost.

There is another ingredient of my bias.

It was early in 1991 when I was reassigned to NASA Headquarters in Washington, DC. I was brought to Headquarters to establish what would become the NASA Academy of Program Project and Engineering Leadership (APPEL). At the time, the objective was to establish a formal and systematic initiative to ensure excellence in programs and projects. Few organizations cared about project management as a discipline worth committing resources for learning, development, and talent management. But NASA, immersed in projects and still recovering from the Challenger disaster, knew it needed to invest in such resources. I was looking to find a good book for distribution in new courses we were designing. The problem was that most books in that time period completely ignored the people and leadership factor in project management. There was a notion that projects were stable, simple activities that required defined tools for planning, scheduling, and controlling the environment. This was a problem, as NASA projects were dynamic, changing, and dependent on effective human interaction. As an organization, we were coming off failed projects due to weaknesses in leadership, communication, and the transfer of knowledge.

It was after a few years of search that I came across a book by Alexander Laufer—*Simultaneous Management: Managing Projects in a Dynamic Environment*. The book was a revelation. It acknowledged that projects were complex undertakings placed within uncertain environments and with a degree of wildness that demanded flexibility, leadership, and an awareness of the human element. With an emphasis on project complexity and change, and calls for adaptive planning, intensive communication, and engaged leadership, the book (and author) became a lifelong source of inspiration for me. The book also hooked me on the power of stories. Throughout it, stories and vignettes were used to powerfully illustrate concepts through real practitioner experience.

It is now 20 years later, and there is another new book that I love—*Becoming a Project Leader: Blending Planning, Agility, Resilience, and Collaboration to Deliver Successful Projects*. It is a collaboration of Alex, Terry, Jeff, and Bruce. These are seasoned practitioners of complex projects, valid and evidence-based research, and leadership. However, it is the wisdom from the book that prompts my strongest reaction. As I mentioned earlier, we live in an age of projects. The world needs exemplary project leaders, and we need project leaders at all levels of an organization and across the entire team spectrum. The challenges we face are too important not to take this seriously; we must stack the deck in favor of excellent results.

Becoming a Project Leader offers principles that increase the probability of project success. Leadership context is provided through the stories of people who actually work on project missions. They are real people struggling with complex situations that require collaborative teamwork, adaptive planning, responsive agility, and proactive resilience. The beauty of projects is that leadership unfolds through people at all places and locations. It is anything but hierarchical. Solutions come from a broad and distributed team, and therefore collective knowledge becomes the defining practice of success. The expertise of a person is not useful unless it is integrated within the total project community. Consider any project: the breadth of expertise and skills covers disparate fields from engineering, science, acquisition, safety, design, systems, and knowledge management. Success is dependent on people collaborating, sharing, arguing, engaging, and integrating. Modern projects are more like orchestras creating beautiful collaborative sounds, as opposed to factories that sequentially produce a part.

Such coordination requires leadership strategies for consistent success. *Becoming a Project Leader* offers several principles that a smart organization will want to employ. First, evolving planning posits a need for project planning that is adaptive and responsive. Learning-based project planning is a critical concept, as project methodology has encountered problems when it becomes focused on control at the exclusion of learning and adaptability. The emphasis on agile and lean methodologies is a reaction against controls that add expense with little learning. Brian Muirhead discusses the danger of formal project reviews that "take an enormous amount of time for the team" and become "a significant distraction; and even worse, a significant loss in momentum." A solution is to benefit from the learning offered from reviews through processes that are flexible and meaningful. In this way planning adds a valued benefit of learning and some sensitivity to the context.

The second principle is responsive agility and places communication as the vital competency for a project leader. If you ask an experienced project manager to identify the most critical competency for leading a project, most will indicate communication. A wonderful example is given in a story about John Hodge, the first leader for the Space Station Task Force. At the early point of my career, I worked for Frank Hoban, a great leader who was a member of the Space Station Task Force, and Frank would share "Hodgie" stories that focused on an environment that was innovative, unstructured, candid, and communication intensive. Successful project managers orchestrate a unique "sound" in which knowledge and passion reverberate without constraint throughout the project team, promoting responsiveness, movement, energy, immediacy, and currency of knowledge. You can hear responsive agility even faster than you can see it.

Third, proactive resilience is about challenging the status quo, proactively and selectively. This may be the most difficult as it requires finding the balance between creative insubordination and blind obedience. We know of cases where projects failed because leadership ignored known problems that required a response different than the planned direction. We also understand there are circumstances where trusting the planned direction has resulted in a positive outcome. How do we handle that balance between planning and improvisation? The authors offer stories and lessons that point to the importance of anticipation, courage, and trusting intuition. Proactive resilience also indicates the importance of responding well and openly to mistakes, mishaps, and failure. I think of a powerful conversation I had with Bryan O'Connor during our time at NASA. Bryan is a leader who inspires. One particular decision of his, which required a courageous stance, prompted me to ask him where he received his courage. He told me about being a young engineer in the room during the ill-fated Challenger Space Shuttle mission. He communicated that there were things not said, things he sensed based on intuition that he should have found his voice to bring up. Out of that lesson he promised to always challenge the situation through communication and honesty.

Collaborative teamwork is the principle that reminds us that performance happens at the team level. This is a simple concept that is often ignored. During the early years of the NASA Academy, we had wonderful training courses, career development, and work assignments for individuals. Then in the late 1990s we had a series of painful failures on Mars missions. At the time the NASA Administrator, Dan Goldin, pointed out (in a very intensive manner) that we had a mature process for individual development but nothing to actually support project teams. In fact, many organizations prepare individuals well, but offer little on preparing project teams. The importance of collaborative teamwork is offered through many stories in *Becoming a Project Leader*, and the description of successful team members by Frank Snow seems particularly relevant. He says the best team members "remained positive and enthusiastic even during project travails. They were very agile, willing to change direction whenever the situation dictated. They were able to subordinate their personal and functional goals to the project's goal. They treated others on the project with respect and were not into blaming others when something went wrong. They were constantly learning and adapting … they were willing to do anything to make the project successful."

Becoming a Project Leader is a wonderful book that offers a way toward project success. It illustrates essential principles of leadership, engagement, and learning. It uses the power of stories to create interest and understanding. You do not have to believe me. Try an exercise. Think of a difficult project. It should be one in which you were an active leader or practitioner. One that had challenges and problems, but that ended successfully. Now ask yourself to tell a story about how the project overcame the challenges to be successful. What are the lessons? What do you believe led to success? My guess is that the concepts of this book will explain your own successes and predict future ones. The stories will resonate and reinforce what you know about excellence in programs and projects.

We live in a world that succeeds and fails at great challenges based on our leadership of programs and projects. We need good project leaders, and we need our project teams to be founded on leadership, engagement, and the ability to learn and learn fast. We need to tell, share, and exchange stories of practitioners. This charming and thoughtful book represents the voice of experienced practitioners and provides a compass for success.

Former NASA Chief Knowledge Officer and   Dr. Edward J. Hoffman
Director NASA Academy
Founder and CEO, Knowledge Engagement
Executive in Residence, Columbia University,
School of Professional Studies

Praise for *Becoming a Project Leader*

This is the project management book we have all been waiting for. We live in an age of projects, and the challenges we face are too important not to take seriously; we need our project teams to be founded on leadership, engagement, and the ability to learn and learn fast. *Becoming a Project Leader* offers several principles that any smart organization will want to employ, principles that lead not just to project success but to a lasting impact on the entire culture of project work.

—Edward J. Hoffman, Former NASA Chief Knowledge Officer and Director, NASA Academy; Founder and CEO, Knowledge Engagement

I love this book! It should be required reading. It shows by real-life examples and explanations how good leaders overcome barriers to project success, and it pushes managers to really think about the organic nature of project teams, which is far more important than following any particular methodology or software development approach. Understanding and living these basic principles of how and why people work together to accomplish miracles is the essence of agile leadership.

—Chuck Walrad, Standards column editor, IEEE *Computer* magazine Editor-in-Chief, Guide to the Enterprise IT Body of Knowledge

Should you ever doubt the critical role communication plays in successful project management, devour this book! Its solid research, apt analogies, and real-world examples make the point all too well: More than your decision-making, lack of communication can kill your project.

—Dianna Booher, author of 47 books, including *What MORE Can I Say? Why Communication Fails and What to Do About It*, and *Creating Personal Presence: Look, Talk, Think, and Act Like a Leader*

Becoming a Project Manager delivers. It delivers practical advice. It delivers real-life examples on every page. It delivers evidence of what works and what doesn't. It delivers sound principles. The decades of experience that the authors bring to this book leaves no doubt that they know what they are writing about. And there is no doubt that you should read and apply the lessons in this book. I highly recommend it.

—Jim Kouzes, the Dean's Executive Fellow of Leadership,
Leavey School of Business, Santa Clara University; and
co-author of the bestselling, *The Leadership Challenge*

Becoming a Project Leader speaks to the realities of managing projects in a world of constant change. One never has perfect information or full awareness of possibilities, so the most effective project leaders enable their teams to plan pragmatically and adjust constantly, while moving the project forward toward the broadly defined outcome. This takes not only organizational skills, but interpersonal and leadership skills that get the right people on the project and build trust among those people.

—Tracy Schroeder, Vice President, Information Services &
Technology, Boston University

Becoming a Project Leader is a must-read for experienced as well as emerging project leaders. It combines a deep study of management and insights into how to make management truly work. As the authors illustrate through research and example, project managers must be individuals who can see around corners, adapt to change, be resilient in the face of adversity, and perhaps most importantly bring out the best in their fellow teammates.

—John Baldoni, internationally acclaimed thought leader, executive coach,
and author of more than a dozen books on leadership, including *MOXIE: The
Secret to Bold and Gutsy Leadership*

Every leader operating in a VUCA [volatility, uncertainty, complexity, and ambiguity] environment needs to read this book. Why? Because it combines research with practice and exemplary models; that is the best coaching you can get from a book. The authors place collaborative teamwork at the heart of the model and combine planning, resilience, and agility to help you improve the quality of your project work. Well worth the read.

—Dr. Eunice Parisi-Carew, co-founder of the Ken Blanchard
Companies and the co-author of three bestselling books: *The One Minute
Manager Builds High Performing Teams, High Five!*, and *Leading at a Higher
Level*

Many books have focused on why projects fail, but this is the first book that uncovers why projects succeed. The difference between projects that succeed and projects that fail comes down to leadership: leadership that inspires individuals toward a vision, builds collaborative teams, steers complex change, and responds to shifting targets. Based on empirical research and valuable from-the-field experience, this extraordinary and insightful book is a must-read, practical guide for anyone involved in complex projects today.

> —Laura McCain Patterson, Associate Vice President
> and Chief Information Officer (Retired), University of Michigan

Becoming a Project Leader is the best sort of management book—combining cases, examples, and theory in an integrated whole which makes for convincing arguments and ease of understanding. This wide-ranging and very up-to-date volume goes a long way in contributing to our need for more pragmatic and innovative project management ideas.

> —Laurence Prusak, Founder and Former Executive Director of the Institute
> for Knowledge Management

Leadership, agility, and adaptation are key themes driving discussion and practice in today's projects and organizations. *Becoming a Project Leader* addresses these themes in a way that seamlessly combines a sound theoretical foundation with practical examples presented as stories so that the entire book is at the same time entertaining and educational. Practitioners will be able to relate to the realities presented in the stories, and the way in which they are presented will help them to make sense of their own experience, enabling them to learn on the job, as this excellent book suggests.

> —Lynn Crawford, Professor of Project Management; Director, Project
> Management Program School of Civil Engineering; Faculty of Engineering
> and Information Technologies, The University of Sydney

In this modern age of project-based business, project management might as well be business management; if your projects don't do well, how can your business possibly do well? Authors Laufer, Little, Russell, and Maas do a great job explaining how understanding a project leader's four simple roles can greatly enhance your ability to manage projects for your organization in that sweet spot right between traditional and agile methods of project management.

> —Chris Hallberg, President, Traction INC.

In its very contemporary analysis of project management, *Becoming a Project Leader* leads to a re-appreciation of many old beliefs, some almost tribal in their origins: the value of direct-contact human relationships, trust, courage, and humility. The authors give significant credit to on-the-job learning and mentorship, and they also provide invaluable insights on the traits common to exceptional project managers and project outcomes.

—Richard M Kunnath, Executive Chairman,
Charles Pankow Builders, Ltd.

Becoming A Project Leader is an excellent read for both experienced and new project managers alike. While there is no substitute for the actual running of a project, this book does a great job capturing the core aspects of a successful project manager and conveys its insights in a clear and reader-friendly way.

—Daniel Barpal, President, Barpal Services, LLC

Becoming a Project Leader is a recipe for success in managing projects in today's rapidly changing work environment—in fact, it redefines management. I found myself sometimes nodding while reading because I could recall a past personal instance where I had luckily used one of the authors' proposed approaches, resulting in a successful outcome. Unfortunately, I also smacked myself in the forehead a few times while reading other chapters. Perhaps some of my past bad experiences could have ended better if I had had the opportunity to read *Becoming a Project Leader* earlier in my career.

—Norma Jean Mattei, 2017 President, American
Society of Civil Engineers

This is a well-researched and detailed book, full of fascinating case studies that bring the project theory to life. It goes beyond the typical project management textbook to help equip project managers for the challenging and shifting circumstances of complex projects. The contextualized stories make it easy for leaders to learn lessons about how best to approach their work; there are practices here that managers can deploy on even the smallest initiatives. Very helpful, and a refreshing read.

—Elizabeth Harrin, Director, Otobos Consultants Ltd.

This is a fabulous book that weaves its way from picking the correct project manager to building your team. It makes a strong case for the importance of communicating, which can be hard for us engineers, who tend to be introverts. It also emphasizes the need to empower people. This book will become a standard for all our budding project managers to read about what works and what does not.

—Robert E. Alger, President & Chief Executive Officer,
Lane Industries, Inc.

Successful projects, as is true of all collaborative efforts, rise and fall on leadership. *Becoming a Project Leader* spells out the art and science of leadership, explaining the four key methods used by top project managers to move from project formation to project implementation. This book provides more than just how-to information, however, for it also inspires by sharing examples of how effective managers utilized the principles to produce results, providing the model for others who aspire to do similarly.

—Orrin Woodward, NY Times Bestselling Author and Inc. Magazine Top 20 Leader

The difference between *Becoming a Project Leader* and other books on this topic is clear from the title. After all, project management is itself an expression of leadership, and the two are interconnected and interdependent. Based on decades of leadership and countless projects, this book is critical for those looking for concrete take-aways and for those looking to understand the difference leadership makes in the practice of project management; something that is not often taught.

—John O'Brien, President and CEO of EDUCAUSE

Becoming a Project Leader is an easy read, using anecdotal short stories to punctuate creative approaches to project management. Rather than present formulaic static rules, the authors' refreshing tack is to encourage the project leader to take on four key roles utilized by successful professionals. Well researched, this book combines the best of proven practices with encouragement to innovative thinking in order to help managers plan and execute successful projects.

—Jim Rispoli, former Assistant Secretary of Energy; Professor of Practice, North Carolina State University

Becoming a Project Leader provides an excellent overview of the basic skill sets required to be successful in today's complex and matrixed organizational structures. While planning skills have traditionally been emphasized by project management leaders, it is most often the softer skills of agility, resilience, and most importantly collaboration that enable successful project outcomes and define outstanding project leaders. *Becoming a Project Leader* is an engaging and instructive treatise on the topic and is a must-read for both experienced and aspiring project leaders.

—John Mullen, Senior Vice President, Dell EMC, NA Commercial Central Field Sales

Becoming a Project Leader is an excellent read that rightly stresses that most of the leadership wisdom needed by the project manager is learned from on-the-job training and experience. The book presents multiple cases enabling the reader to benefit from the rich experience of successful Project Managers and from in-depth reflections on this experience. It is truly unique, a must-read for all project managers.

—William W. Badger, Professor Emeritus, Arizona State University

Preface

Becoming a Project Leader arises out of a passion for competent leadership in action. When a team of capable, knowledgeable people led by a successful project manager tackle a project, it seems there's nothing they can't accomplish. The authors of this book have all seen teams surmount enormous obstacles, deftly handling unforeseen problems, and, ultimately, taking joy in the work and exceeding expectations. This book comes from a desire to understand how the project leader, the hub of such well-oiled machines, can orchestrate such miracles.

There's a certain sorcery to the successful project manager's success. The position requires a unique combination of judgment, interpersonal skills, and an ability to assimilate information quickly. It's easy to believe that such sorcery cannot be taught, that you either have it or you don't. Certainly, education in project management has more often than not missed the mark. But through their combined 140 years of research and practice, the authors have lived, seen, helped create, and studied exactly what it is that the best project managers do.

Nowadays, project management is essential across all industries. It has always been associated with manufacturing and construction—and indeed, there's a lot to be learned from such industries. But project management and the shared traits of successful project managers are now crucial in Information Technology, Education, Healthcare, Government, and Entertainment. All startups are projects. Consequently, this is a book both for those who know they're in project management and those who know only that they need to organize a lot of people (who don't normally work together) to accomplish a unique goal.

The four authors of *Becoming a Project Leader* have not only studied and reflected upon project successes but been actively involved in leading projects themselves and consulting with managers. They come from a wide variety of industries, including information technology, military, product development, space projects, and construction. They've also all been active in educating leaders, and so they're well aware of the shortcomings of professional development and leadership training; *Becoming a Project Leader* comes from a desire to create a practical guide to project management.

The authors are indebted to countless people for the content of this book. Within these pages is a collection of wisdom coming from a vast and diverse array of wonderful people, who exhibited not just competence in their leadership, not just excellence in their fields, but also a tremendous generosity of spirit in their willingness to share their wisdom. Successful project managers know more than they think they know. And it was the authors' pleasure to mine that knowledge in order to create *Becoming a Project Leader*.

Madison, Wisconsin, USA   Alexander Laufer
Haifa, Israel

Fairfax Station, Virginia, USA   Terry Little

Madison, Wisconsin, USA   Jeffrey Russell

Madison, Wisconsin, USA   Bruce Maas

Acknowledgments

First and foremost, we owe our gratitude to our teachers over the years—some of whom knew they were instructing us and some of whom had no idea. Those we interviewed, those we worked with, those who mentored us, those we mentored or advised, those at any level of the work whose competence impressed us—all were our teachers. It was our job to uncover both the explicit and the tacit knowledge of people immersed in and adept at project work. Excellence is the best teacher. And we're forever grateful for these excellent role models. We're grateful, too, to the many companies over the years who have welcomed us and challenged us, including NASA, Proctor & Gamble, the US Air Force, Motorola, Turner Construction Company, the Boldt Group, and the University of Wisconsin-Madison.

We are also indebted to those who helped us put together this book. Those who reviewed drafts gave us insightful suggestions and provided probing questions to push us toward clearer and/or more in-depth explanation. In addition, we got valuable feedback and encouragement from our dozens of endorsers, whose expertise we admire and whose esteem we cherish. Barry Carlsen, who did our illustrations, provided tremendous help with our tables and figures, putting an artistic stamp on our concepts. Tim Storm provided invaluable editing; not only did he polish our phrasing, often pushing us toward more consistent and more incisive analysis and offering fluid rewrites of passages, but he served as a sort of creative director for the entire manuscript. And Stephen Partridge, Editorial Director, Business, Economics, and Finance at Palgrave Macmillan, helped us make this project a reality, pushing us toward a more engaging book.

Bruce Maas owes his gratitude to the University of Wisconsin for providing him with opportunities to grow throughout his career. His work with a diverse array of students, faculty, and colleagues across the country has encouraged him never to lose sight of the people behind the technology.

Jeffrey Russell would like to thank the taxpayers of Wisconsin, the University of Wisconsin-Madison, and his colleagues for the opportunity to learn and teach in the project management area, and for students who have taught him through their questions and curiosity; he would also like to thank the industry professionals (Boldt Company, J.H. Findorff & Sons, J.P. Cullen & Sons, J.F. Ahern Company, Mortenson Construction, Pieper Electric, Affiliated Engineers) who have taken time to teach, encourage, and mentor him in the project management area.

Terry Little is indebted to the United States Department of Defense for providing him with an enormous variety of project experience. Those he mentored, those he worked with, and those he led—all helped him learn that leadership is a matter of serving and supporting others while helping achieve a broader organizational mission.

Alexander Laufer would like to thank the many companies that opened their doors to him and the countless practitioners who were willing to share their expertise and insights. He has been blessed with a career that has allowed him to travel far and wide, listening to and drawing out the stories of some remarkable people.

Finally, we all owe our most gratitude to our families, whose support throughout the years has enabled us to pursue our passions for project management and education. There's no question that Alex Laufer was the captain of this ship, and his wife Yochy is and has always been the wind in the sails. Her support of this project and of Alex was evident to all.

Contents

About the Authors

Alexander Laufer is the Director of the Consortium for Project Leadership at the University of Wisconsin-Madison, an industry consultant, and Chaired Professor of Civil Engineering at the Technion—Israel Institute of Technology. He has served as the editor-in-chief of *Academy Sharing Knowledge*, the NASA Academy of Program and Project Leadership magazine, and as a member of the advisory board of the NASA Academy of Program and Project Leadership. He has also served as the Director of the Center for Project Leadership at Columbia University. Laufer is the author or co-author of six books; the two most recent ones are *Mastering the Leadership Role in Project Management: Practices that Deliver Remarkable Results* (2012) and *Breaking the Code of Project Management* (Macmillan, 2009). He has significant consulting experience and has worked with a number of leading organizations, including Boldt, Motorola, NASA, Parsons Brinckerhoff, Procter & Gamble, Skanska, and Turner Construction Company.

Terry Little was the Department of Defense's (DoD) most seasoned manager of major programs, with more than 25 years' experience leading major weapons acquisitions. Also one of the department's most forceful advocates for program management innovation, Little is considered by many to be the best program manager in recent DoD history. Currently, he consults on acquisition leadership and business development with The Spectrum Group and with Modern Technology Solutions. An honorary professor at the Defense Systems Management College, Little has presented case studies to every program manager class at the college for the past 15 years. Little served as Executive Director of the Missile Defense Agency—the senior civilian in an organization of approximately 8000 employees—while also directing the $14 billion Kinetic Energy Interceptor Program. Previously, he was the first director of the Air Force Acquisition Center of Excellence, which enhanced all acquisition activities through streamlining contracts, devising incentives, and overseeing contractors. Little's many awards include the Secretary of Defense Meritorious Civilian Service

Award (received twice), the Executive Service Presidential Rank Award, and the Air Force Stewart Award for Excellence in Program Management. He holds an MS in Systems Analysis from the Air Force Institute of Technology and an MBA from the University of West Florida. After graduating with distinction from Officer Training School in 1967, he served eight years in active duty with the US Air Force.

Jeffrey S. Russell is Vice Provost for Lifelong Learning, Dean of Continuing Studies, and Executive Director of the Consortium for Project Management at the University of Wisconsin-Madison. In his role as vice provost and dean, he is responsible for leading the university's programs and services for lifelong learners and nontraditional students. Russell has earned a reputation as a leader in innovative project delivery systems. He is a respected researcher, author, and editor. He has written more than 200 technical papers in the areas of contractor failure, prequalification, surety bonds, constructability, automation, maintainability, warranties, and quality control/quality assurance. In addition, he has authored and written two books: *Constructor Prequalification* (1996) and *Surety Bonds for Construction Contracts* (2000). And he has served as editor-in-chief of the *Journal of Management in Engineering* and as founding editor-in-chief of *Leadership and Management in Engineering*. Russell has been honored with over 20 national and regional awards and 9 best paper awards. His recent awards include Distinguished Membership of the American Society of Civil Engineers (ASCE) in 2009, being elected to the National Academy of Construction (NAC) in 2011, and being elected as Fellow of the National Society of Professional Engineers (NSPE) in 2011.

Bruce Maas is Emeritus Vice Provost for Information Technology and Chief Information Officer (CIO) at the University of Wisconsin-Madison, a position he has held since August 2011. Prior to that, he served for seven years as the CIO at the University of Wisconsin-Milwaukee. Maas has served as the director of the EDUCAUSE Leadership Institute, the leading professional association for information technology in higher education, and he is presently serving as the board chair. He is also a member of the Internet2 External Relations PAG and Co-Chair of the Internet2 Global Summit Planning Committee. In addition, he is a member of the Board of Directors of Unizin and is serving a three-year term on the Board of Directors of IMS Global. Maas holds an MS in Administrative Leadership from the University of Wisconsin-Milwaukee as well as bachelor degrees in Accounting and Management Information Systems (MIS).

List of Figures

List of Tables

1

Leading the Project from Living Order to Geometric Order

"Thinking well is wise; planning well is wiser; doing well wisest and best of all."
Persian Proverb

All White-Collar Work Today Is Project Work

Whereas the Industrial Revolution emphasized skill and task specialization, the current information revolution is generating greater task complexity, which demands the integration of a diverse set of skills. In the mid-1990s, such demands led to the use of the project method as the predominant management strategy for structuring organizations and defining the roles and tasks of mid-level managers [1, 2].

Projects are defined as temporary endeavors undertaken to create a unique product or service. A project may be as simple as the plan for an off-site retreat or as complex as the development and production of a space shuttle. In the project method, instead of people being grouped in the traditional functional units based on common means (skills, work processes, or knowledge), they are grouped in cross-functional units based on the project's goals. The project culture, which fosters responsiveness to customers, has enabled organizations to easily migrate from the producer-dominated market of yesterday to the more complex customer-driven market of today.

With the growing recognition that the project method is the keystone of modern organizations, most managers in today's companies spend much of their time focusing on projects. As Tom Peters stated in 1999, "All white-collar

© The Author(s) 2018
A. Laufer et al., *Becoming a Project Leader*,
https://doi.org/10.1007/978-3-319-66724-9_1

work today is project work" [3]. And as Rolf A. Lundin and his colleagues stated in 2015, "The projectification of business and working life is ongoing and strong. This movement goes beyond traditional project-organized sectors such as construction, consultancy, media, and entertainment. Project thinking is spreading to most parts of society, including industrial enterprises, governmental organizations, educational institutions, and volunteer groups" [4].

The Poor Statistics of Project Results

Paradoxically, the sharp increase in the popularity of the project method has been accompanied by an increasing dissatisfaction with current project management results. As succinctly and painfully summarized by the opening statement of a 2007 article in the *Harvard Business Review*, "Projects fail at a spectacular rate" [5]. This point was emphatically remade in a recent issue of the same journal: "Why don't most project managers sound the alarm when they're going to blow past their deadlines? Because most of them have no earthly idea when they'll finish the job. They don't even think it's possible to know" [6].

The Standish Group has been doing surveys on all types of IT projects since 1994. Its 2014 report shares this alarming finding:

"The Standish Group research shows a staggering 31.1% of projects will be cancelled before they ever get completed. Further results indicate 52.7% of projects will cost 189% of their original estimates. The cost of these failures and overruns are just the tip of the proverbial iceberg. The lost opportunity costs are not measurable, but could easily be in the trillions of dollars. One just has to look to the City of Denver to realize the extent of this problem. The failure to produce reliable software to handle baggage at the new Denver airport is costing the city $1.1 million per day" [7].

Such poor results are not limited to IT projects. For example, a Rand Corporation study that examined 52 extremely large projects found that the projects suffered from an average cost growth of 88% [8]. A recent study that examined ten large rail-transit projects in the United States found that the projects suffered from an average cost overrun of 61%, while the average cost overrun of eight large road projects in Sweden was 86% [9]. Finally, a study by PricewaterhouseCoopers that reviewed 10,640 projects from 200 companies in 30 countries across various industries found that only 2.5% of the companies successfully completed 100% of their projects [10].

Developing Project Management Knowledge: Learning from Practice

---

》The overall objective of our research has been to bridge the gap between research and practice by developing practice-based principles for managing projects

---

Many researchers have concluded that an important reason for the widespread poor results of projects is the wide gap between research and practice [11–14]. The overall objective of our research has been to bridge this gap by developing practice-based principles for managing projects. Believing that management is best learned by emulating exemplary role models, we've based this book on more than two decades of research that has attempted to capture the proven practices of some of the most competent project managers. Toward this end, we've used multiple, complementary approaches to collect firsthand data on the practices of successful project managers, focusing our studies on a selective sample of the best practitioners in leading organizations (Table 1.1). Our research methodologies were influenced in many respects by the well-known management scholar, Henry Mintzberg, who stresses the use of systematic observations of managers [15, 16].

Our first approach consisted of field studies and structured research tools, which included two-to-four-hour interviews and up to one-week-long observations of practitioners from various organizations such as AT&T, Bechtel, DuPont, General Motors, IBM, Motorola, PPL Electric Utilities, Procter & Gamble, and Turner Construction Company. Our second approach involved facilitating reflective dialogues among project team members. We collected most of the cases, stories, and practices through our role as the facilitators of

Table 1.1 The various research methods employed in putting together this book

Approach	Rationale
Interviews and observations	Management is best learned by emulating exemplary project managers
Dialogues in knowledge-sharing communities	Meaningful reflection—key for learning about best practices—can often be facilitated in collaborative story-sharing
Consulting engagements	Principles learned through the above methods must be put to the test

the project management knowledge-development and knowledge-sharing communities in three organizations: NASA (five years), Procter & Gamble (three years), and Boldt (two years). Overall, more than 150 project managers from over 20 organizations participated in our studies [17–19]. To make sure the principles we developed were a valid interpretation of the stories we had collected, we adopted a third approach: testing our interim results in real-life situations through consulting engagements.

From Living Order to Geometric Order

Employing our practice-based research approach, we have identified two primary reasons for the poor outcomes of projects: the degree of unexpected events plaguing today's projects and the prevalent either/or approaches to project management.

About 2500 years ago, the Greek philosopher Heraclitus argued that the only constant in our world is change. Today, rapid technological innovations as well as the economic, social, and political challenges of globalization make this statement as true as ever. Peter Vaill, an American professor of management, has compared functioning in the complex, turbulent, and changing environment faced by today's organizational leaders to navigating in "permanent white water" [20].

In using this metaphor, Vaill was calling attention to the fact that the external environment of contemporary projects is full of surprises, tends to produce novel problems, and is "messy" and ill-structured. However, it was the French Nobel Prize winner Henri Bergson who, a century ago, proposed a concept of order that may help us better understand project reality today. In his 1907 book *Creative Evolution*, Bergson claimed that there is no such thing as disorder. Instead, there are two sorts of order: geometric order and living order (see Fig. 1.1). The former, according to Bergson, relates to the traditional concept of order in which events are well organized and predictable. The latter, living order, refers to phenomena that might not seem orderly but represent the natural order of events and objects as they evolve [21].

All project managers strive to reach their project objectives by relying on processes characterized by geometric order. However, in our studies, which are substantiated by many other recent studies, we have found that project managers must frequently cope with numerous unexpected events. These can range from everyday occurrences, such as the failure of a worker to show up or changes in a customer's requirements, to rarer events, such as the bankruptcy of a key vendor. Such unexpected events often disrupt the orderly

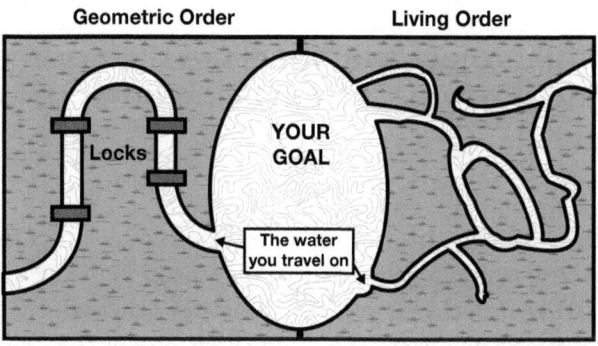

Fig. 1.1 Geometric order is organized and predictable, like a canal; living order is turbulent and changing, like a natural river

progress of the project. Maintaining projects in geometric order becomes impossible as projects are transformed to living order. Coping with the challenging living order of the project becomes the primary role of the project manager [22–27].

In a world perceived as being in "geometric order," projects require only plan-driven *management*. However, in the real world of "living order," where unexpected events are inevitable, there is a need for both management and *leadership*. Most of any project's problems can be solved with knowledge and procedures already at hand and termed *technical problems* by Ronald Heifetz from Harvard University. Although solving these problems may require great flexibility and high responsiveness, they can still be resolved while *maintaining the status quo*. They just require good *managerial* skills. Other problems, however, are *adaptive*—that is, they are not so well defined, do not have clear solutions, and often require fundamental changes in patterns of behavior. In order to address these adaptive problems, Heifetz asserts, the project manager must be willing to *challenge the status quo*, which calls for *leadership* [28].

The two management approaches most frequently employed by project managers are the so-called traditional approach and the agile approach. The traditional approach assumes that project success can be achieved by focusing on planning, controlling, and managing risks. Thus, this approach largely ignores the need to cope with numerous unexpected events and their negative impact on the project's plans. The traditional approach is based on the assumption that project processes will follow geometric order [29]. In contrast, one of the principles of the agile approach (indeed its veritable "manifesto") is "responding to change over following a plan." The assumption underlying this approach is that the living order dominates to the point that it is not advisable to spend time on planning with the goal of reaching geometric order.

❯❯ Successful project managers see their primary role as leading the project from living order to geometric order

The literature assumes that project managers employ either the traditional approach or the agile approach—that is, they are either driven by geometric order or by living order. Our research indicates otherwise. Observing and working with project managers, we found that one of the hallmarks of the more successful ones is that they employ a hybrid of the traditional and the agile approaches. While they acknowledge the need to constantly cope with unexpected events, at the same time they attempt to plan and control the project. And at times they have to cope with adaptive problems and to assume a leadership role. These project managers see their primary role as leading the project from living order to geometric order.

Employing a hybrid of the traditional and agile practices is more challenging and complex than following one approach or the other. Thus, developing a guide for practitioners requires special attention to simplicity [30]. During the last decade we focused on developing and testing, in real-life situations, a simple guide suitable for today's dynamic environment. The guide focuses on the four key roles of the project leader, as outlined in the next section.

The Four Roles of the Project Leader

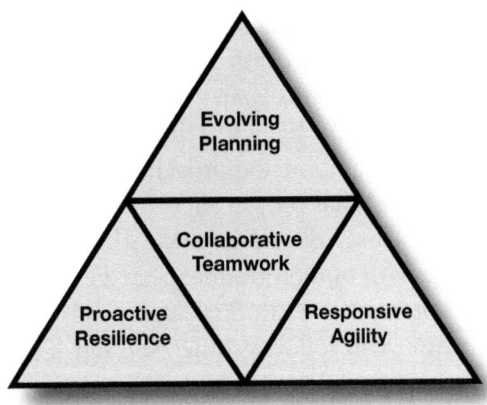

In our efforts to intellectualize practice, we were able to identify the four key roles employed by successful project managers. The first three roles—planning, agility, and resilience—focus on coping with changes, with each role relating to a different kind of change. These three roles, which complement each other, can be implemented effectively only when they are supported by the fourth role, collaboration.

The first role, **planning** (covered in Chap. 2), evolves throughout the life of the project and is typically employed at weekly-to-quarterly planning sessions in order to cope with changes that are identified periodically. The project manager coordinates and integrates this evolving process, ensuring that the project team develops stable short-term plans and flexible long-term plans and conducts learning-based project reviews. The second role, **agility** (covered in Chap. 3), is exercised continuously to cope with frequent unexpected events. Here, in order to maintain forward momentum, the project manager is action oriented, responding with agility to problems as soon as they are identified. The third role, **resilience** (covered in Chap. 4), is applied only occasionally. In this role, the project manager proactively handles major problems that may lead to significant project disruptions.

In a typical project, coping with unexpected events is challenging due to the unique, temporary, and evolving project organization that is composed of heterogeneous units. Detecting problems in a timely manner and coping with them quickly and effectively becomes even more challenging if the various parties do not collaborate. Thus, in the fourth role (covered in Chap. 5), the project manager develops and maintains **collaborative teamwork** by selecting the right people and by developing interdependence and trust among them.

Becoming a Project Leader: Learning from Experience

》The objective of the manager should be to become a practitioner by learning from practice and not by learning about practice

---

Prominent researchers have argued for more than a quarter of a century that the objective of the manager should be to become a practitioner by learning **from** practice and not by learning **about** practice [31–33]. As explained by Henry Mintzberg, "Management is not a science. ... Most management is a craft, meaning that it relies on experience—learning on the job. ... Put

Table 1.2 A preview of the topics covered throughout the book

Topic	Definition	Chapter
Planning (the first role)	An evolving process which includes stable short-term plans and flexible long-term plans, as well as learning-based project reviews	2
Agility (the second role)	The ability to respond to frequent unexpected events as soon as they are identified	3
Resilience (the third role)	The ability to proactively handle major problems that may lead to significant project disruptions	4
Collaborative teamwork (the fourth role)	Selecting the right people and developing interdependence and trust among them	5
On-the-job learning	Management must be learned from experience and facilitated by challenging assignments, mentoring, and reflections through communities of practice	6
Project context	There is no "one best way"; project decisions must be tailored to context	7

together a good deal of craft with a certain amount of art and some science, and you end up with a job that is above all a *practice*" [34].

Real-life stories and case studies can serve as partial substitutes for experience [35–37]. However, sharing stories is not sufficient. Project managers need to "learn how to learn" from experience, and this is the focus of Chap. 6 of the book, "On-the-Job-Learning," where we discuss how learning from experience can be facilitated by challenging assignments, mentoring, and reflections through communities of practice.

The prevailing theories of project management have failed to give sufficient explicit treatment to the unique context of the project and have, at least implicitly, embraced the "one best way" philosophy. Peter Drucker maintains that the "one best way" assumptions underlying the discipline of management are "totally at odds with reality and … totally counterproductive" [38]. This important issue will be addressed in Chap. 7. For a summary of the topics covered throughout the book, see Table 1.2.

Key Points

- The project method is the predominant strategy for most modern work, which relies on cross-functional units based on project goals.
- But projects fail at an alarming rate.
- Such failure springs in part from the large gap between research and practice; the methodologies used to create this book bridge that gap.

- Successful project managers employ both traditional and agile approaches to wrangle chaotic, living order and create more geometric order.
- This book promotes a combination of four roles—planning, agility, resilience, and collaborative teamwork—as necessary for successful project management.
- The successful project manager must learn from practice, not about practice.

References

1. Price Waterhouse Change Integration Team. *The Paradox Principles: How High Performance Companies Manage Chaos, Complexity and Contradictions to Achieve Superior Results*. 1996, Chicago: Irwin Professional Publisher.
2. Stewart, T.A. The Corporate Jungle Spawns a New Species: The Project Manager. *Fortune* 1995; July: p. 179–180.
3. Peters, T. The Wow project. *Fast Company* 1999; April(24): p. 116.
4. Lundin, R.A., Arvidsson, N., Brady, T., Ekstedt, E., Midler, C., and Sydow, J. *Managing and Working in Project Society*. 2015, Cambridge: Cambridge University Press.
5. Klein, G. Performing a Project Premortem. *Harvard Business Review* 2007; 85(9): p. 18–19.
6. Knight, J., Thomas, R., and Angus, B. The Dirty Little Secret of Project Management. *Harvard Business Review* 2013; https://hbr.org/2013/03/the-dirty-little-secret-of-pro#, (accessed 2016).
7. *The Standish Group Report Chaos*. 2014; https://www.projectsmart.co.uk/white-papers/chaos-report.pdf, (accessed 2016).
8. Merrow, E. and Merrow, E.W. *Understanding the Outcomes of Mega-Projects*. 1988, Santa Monica, CA: Rand Corporation.
9. Flyvbjerg, B., Bruzelius, N., and Rothengatter, W. *Megaprojects and Risk: An Anatomy of Ambition*. 2003, Cambridge: Cambridge University Press.
10. Hardy-Vallee, B. The Cost of Bad Project Management. *Gallup Business Journal* 2012; http://www.gallup.com/businessjournal/152429/cost-bad-project-management, (accessed 2016).
11. Cicmil, S., Williams, T., Thomas, J., and Hodgson, D. Rethinking Project Management: Researching the Actuality of Projects. *International Journal of Project Management* 2006; 24(8): p. 675–686.
12. Koskela, L. and Howell, G. The Underlying Theory of Project Management Is Obsolete, in *Proceedings of the PMI Research Conference*. 2002; Project Management Institute.
13. Lenfle, S. and Loch, C. Lost Roots: How Project Management Came to Emphasize Control over Flexibility and Novelty. *California Management Review* 2010; 53(1): p. 32–55.

14. Söderland, J., Geraldi, J., and Engwall, M. PERT, Polaris, and the Realities of Project Execution. *International Journal of Managing Projects in Business* 2012; 5(4): p. 595–616.

15. Feldman, M.S. and Orlikowski, W.J. Theorizing Practice and Practicing Theory. *Organization Science* 2011; 22(5): p. 1240–1253.

16. Mintzberg, H. Developing Theory About the Development of Theory, in *Great Minds in Management: The Process of Theory Development*, K. Smith and M. Hitt, Editors. 2005, New York: Oxford University Press: p. 355–372.

17. Brown, J.S. Narrative as a Knowledge Medium in Organizations, in *Storytelling in Organizations: Why Storytelling Is Transforming 21st Century Organizations and Management*, J.S. Brown, S. Denning, K. Groh, and L. Prusak, Editors. 2005, London: Routledge: p. 53–95.

18. Lee, D., Simmons, J., and Drueen, J. Knowledge Sharing in Practice: Applied Storytelling and Knowledge Communities at NASA. *International Journal of Knowledge and Learning* 2005; 1(1–2): p. 171–180.

19. Wenger, E., McDermott, R., and Snyder, W.M. *Cultivating Communities of Practice*. 2002, Boston: Harvard Business School Press.

20. Vaill, P.B. *Learning as a Way of Being: Strategies for Survival in a World of Permanent White Water*. 1996, San Francisco: Jossey-Bass.

21. Bergson, H. *Creative Evolution*. 1944, New York: Random House.

22. Aaltonen, K., Kujala, J., Lehtonen, P., and Ruuska, I. A Stakeholder Network Perspective on Unexpected Events and Their Management in International Projects. *International Journal of Managing Projects in Business* 2010; 3(4): p. 564–588.

23. Geraldi, J.G., Lee-Kelley, L., and Kutsch, E. The Titanic Sunk, So What? Project Manager Response to Unexpected Events. *International Journal of Project Management* 2010; 28(6): p. 547–558.

24. Hällgren, M. and Maaninen-Olsson, E. Deviations and the Breakdown of Project Management Principles. *International Journal of Managing Projects in Business* 2009; 2(1): p. 53–69.

25. Holmberg, I., Tyrstrup, M., and Tengblad, S. Managerial Leadership as Event-Driven Improvisation, in *The Work of Managers: Towards a Practice Theory of Management*, S. Tengblad, Editor. 2012, Oxford: Oxford University Press: p. 47–68.

26. Söderholm, A. Project Management of Unexpected Events. *International Journal of Project Management* 2008; 26(1): p. 80–86.

27. Styhre, A. Leadership as Muddling Through: Site Managers in the Construction Industry, in *The Work of Managers: Towards a Practice Theory of Management*, S. Tengblad, Editor. 2012, Oxford: Oxford University Press: p. 131–145.

28. Heifetz, R.A. *Leadership Without Easy Answers*. 1994, Cambridge: Harvard University Press.

29. Boehm, B. and Turner, R. *Balancing Agility and Discipline: A Guide for the Perplexed*. 2004, Boston: Pearson Education, Inc.

30. De Bono, E. *Simplicity*. 1999, London: Penguin
31. Brown, J.S. and Duguid, P. Organizational Learning and Communities-of-Practice: Toward a Unified View of Working, Learning, and Innovation. *Organization Science* 1991; 2(1): p. 40–57.
32. McCall, M.W. *High Flyers: Developing the Next Generation of Leaders*. 1998, Cambridge: Harvard Business School Press.
33. McCall, M.W., Lombardo, M.M., and Morrison, A.M. *Lessons of Experience: How Successful Executives Develop on the Job*. 1988, New York: Simon and Schuster.
34. Mintzberg, H. *Managers, Not MBAs: A Hard Look at the Soft Practice of Managing and Management Development*. 2004, Oakland, CA: Berrett-Koehler Publishers.
35. Laufer, A. *Breaking the Code of Project Management*. 2009, New York: Palgrave Macmillan.
36. Laufer, A. *Mastering the Leadership Role in Project Management: Practices that Deliver Remarkable Results*. 2012, New Jersey: FT Press.
37. Laufer, A., Hoffman, E.J., Russell, J.S., and Cameron, W.S. What Successful Project Managers Do. *MIT Sloan Management Review* 2015; 56(3): p. 43–51.
38. Drucker, P.F. *Management Challenges for the 21st Century*. 1999, New York: HarperCollins.

2

The Planning Practice: Employ an Evolving Process

"It is a bad plan that admits of no modification."
Publilius Syrus

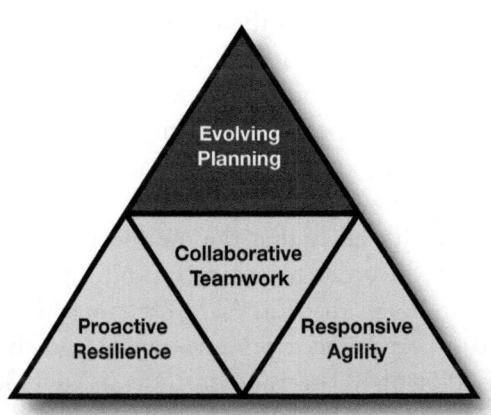

Project planning fulfills multiple purposes, including setting project objectives, providing the guidelines for project implementation, and providing a yardstick for monitoring project implementation. In today's dynamic environment, when projects are initiated with incomplete knowledge and missing information and the project's team has to cope with frequent changes, how can useful plans be developed? In this chapter, we will discuss the practices employed by successful project leaders for developing appropriate objectives and effective plans that will enable them to reach those objectives.

© The Author(s) 2018
A. Laufer et al., *Becoming a Project Leader*,
https://doi.org/10.1007/978-3-319-66724-9_2

Finalize the Formulation of Project Objectives as You Try to Reach Them

The prevailing belief is that "the starting point for any project is to get a clear description of the goal." Does the practice of successful project managers support this assumption? [1] Following are examples of real cases that shed light on this issue.

The ATM Exercise

A mix of highly experienced and novice project managers at a NASA seminar were asked to play the role of a project customer and define four specific objectives for new software that would be used with an Automated Teller Machine (ATM). While the more experienced managers defined the objectives succinctly, using one-word terms such as "functionality," "reliability," "security," and "user friendly," the less-experienced project managers' objectives were elaborate and detailed. Thus, for example, instead of "functionality," they wrote: "Provide money in the form of $20s with no fee and warn Home Office of empty condition at least one hour in advance of becoming empty." And instead of "user-friendly," they wrote: "The ATM accepts at least 10 major credit cards and operates in 6 major languages with complete instructions provided where a withdrawal transaction, including printing the receipt, occurs in less than 60 seconds" [2].

Why this difference? It's likely that the more experienced managers purposely remained vague in order to avoid committing too early to specific objectives. Research indicates that this ATM exercise faithfully represents the practices employed by experienced project managers in the real world. For example, an examination of 308 decision processes in West Germany unequivocally demonstrated that the objective-formation process was not completed before the beginning of the problem-solving activity [3]. Similarly, a study of 211 R&D projects found that the extent to which project objectives were well defined at the time of initiation was not significantly related to the project's eventual success or failure. What made the difference between successful and unsuccessful projects was how well the objectives were defined *later* in the life of the project [4].

This holds true not only in R&D projects where incomplete knowledge and missing information are predominant throughout project life. In a study in which 39 experienced project managers involved in the design and construction of manufacturing plants at 11 large US corporations were interviewed, it became obvious that these project managers did not adhere to the rule "define the problem, then solve it" or "objectives first, means second." Rather, in almost all the 39 projects the objective-specification process was not an isolated activity, and it was not completed before the search for alternative means began. Formulating all the objectives was often completed only during the design phase of the project, and at times even later [5].

Managing Goals

》in a dynamic environment, formulation of objectives must be bound up with action in an interactive and continuous process

---

James March and Henry Mintzberg, two prominent researchers who conducted extensive research on decision making and planning, justify this practice and provide the rationale for it. James March concludes, "The argument that goal development and choice are independent behaviorally seems clearly false. It seems to me perfectly obvious that a description that assumes that goals come first and action comes later is frequently radically wrong. Human choice behavior is as much a process for discovering goals as for acting on them" [6]. Henry Mintzberg concludes that in a dynamic environment, "thought" (formulation of goals) does not simply guide "action" (implementation of these goals). Rather, in a dynamic environment, formulation of objectives must be bound up with action in an interactive and continuous process, so that "learning" becomes the essence of the process of formulating objectives [7].

Now we are better equipped to reflect on and understand the opening story regarding the level of detail in the requirements given for an ATM machine, which presented striking differences between experienced and junior project managers. The experienced project managers sensed that because the scenario was posed at the beginning of the conceptual phase of their task, it was advisable to first examine the means rather than immediately attempt to formulate the requirements in great detail. In essence, they blended the formulation of the requirements with the examination of the means [8] (Fig. 2.1).

Indeed, the key is not to rush and finalize the formulation of project objectives too early. As the early phases of planning are taking place and the cus-

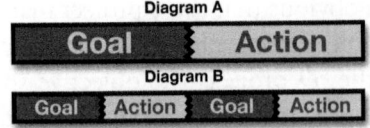

Fig. 2.1   Rather than formulate the entirety of the goal/requirements and then fit the action perfectly to that goal (Diagram **A**), effective project managers formulate objectives in an interactive and continuous process (Diagram **B**)

tomers are exposed to various conceptual solutions and alternatives, they are often able to further develop their ideas of what they really want as well as what they can afford. However, at times, "not rushing" is not enough, and the project managers may take a more proactive role in their attempt to finalize project objectives. Following are two examples that highlight the contribution of such proactive approaches.

Proactive Approaches

Five companies competed for the contract of the US Air Force Joint Air-to-Surface Standoff Missile (JASSM) program. Terry Little, the project manager, who was brought in to this floundering project, was expected, as his first duty, to provide the companies with the objectives (requirements) that would guide the preparation of their proposals. However, Little believed it was too much to expect the customer (i.e., the US Air Force) to clearly know, in total and final detail, what it wanted before briefing the designers. Therefore, for the first three months, he held weekly update meetings with representatives from each of the five companies, engaging them in the process of formulating the project's objectives by asking them for feedback. He encouraged them to tell him what they believed were realistic objectives. Which were consistent with getting a low-cost operational system? Were they spinning their wheels in some area that they didn't really understand? A couple of the companies said that with the requirements defined as they were, it would take a really long time to go through all the engineering details necessary to design a missile that would fit all planes. Instead, they suggested putting it only on one or two planes, getting it built and fielded, and only then modifying the missile for other planes, if necessary. Their suggestion was "Give us a problem that we can work, and then add this additional scope." As summarized by Terry Little:

We sometimes have a problem in that we establish a requirement (objective) without understanding what it really means to try and satisfy that requirement. Until you understand the implications of what you are asking for, in terms of what it costs and how it affects schedule, it can't possibly be a firm requirement. The fact of the matter is that most requirements are just things someone made up. It starts off as somebody's opinion or view of what would be good; but what often happens is that everybody then begins to march as if it's a law of nature that you've got to meet this requirement. However much time it takes, and however much money it takes, it doesn't matter because the requirement is the requirement [9].

Terry's decision to bring the contractors in on the objective-formation process allowed him to avoid arbitrary requirements and their ensuing costs and time. And the advice he got, to initially fit just one or two planes, is in keeping with another bit of wisdom about establishing objectives: prototype [10].

At times, creating a real, one-to-one model of a project's critical elements and physically engaging the users with the model may allow them to learn directly and quickly what they really need. While this process consumes time and resources, it ensures valid and reliable feedback from the users, and in the final analysis it brings about the early completion of stable requirements that require few changes.

This approach was adopted to define the requirements for the interior design of the corporate headquarters building of Procter & Gamble in downtown Cincinnati. The large number of new offices that were planned meant, for example, that one mistake in the workstation design would be potentially repeated 3000 or more times. The team decided that their best bet was to create a mock-up of the building's interior, and that by engaging the users they would be able to learn and define the specific project objectives. They rented the entire sixth floor of a building within walking distance of the existing corporate headquarters that had the same column-bay spacing as was planned for the new building. The team constructed different furniture systems, decorating them with a variety of carpets, paints, lighting schemes, and window treatments. They had people "occupy" the various office mock-ups in order to collect early feedback on the different settings. As the models were built, the design team developed cost and schedule implications for each design option. Finally, the customers were invited for several cycles of reviews and mock-up changes resulting from their feedback. The final decisions regarding interior design requirements were made once the customers fully understood the end product and its cost and schedule implications and were satisfied with them [11].

Employ the Rolling Wave Approach to Plan Project Implementation

Planning is a decision-making process whereby interdependent decisions are integrated into a system of decisions. What makes effective planning implementation particularly challenging is that planning entails an anticipatory decision-making process, as decisions are made on what and how to perform future actions. However, in today's dynamic environment, characterized by frequent unexpected events and volatile information, anticipation becomes very difficult, and the key question faced by the project team is how far in advance of implementation they should make their decisions. Making them early provides more time to develop and coordinate these decisions with other interrelated decisions, and in general, to be better prepared for implementation. However, if decisions are made too early, there is a high probability that the changes that will take place between the time of decision making and the time of implementation will require that the decisions be modified.

Today's successful project managers cope with these conflicting considerations by employing a "rolling wave" approach to planning. Recognizing that long-term firm commitments cannot be made on the basis of volatile information, they develop plans in waves as the project unfolds and information becomes more reliable. With their teams, they develop Action Plans, which are detailed short-term plans with firm commitments. They also prepare medium-term plans (e.g., 90-day Look-Ahead Plans), which are less detailed in comparison, and long-term plans (Master Plans), which cover the duration of the entire project and are quite general, presenting only aggregate activities. This way, they can ensure short-term stability and long-term flexibility.

As shown in Fig. 2.2, Action Plans with a one-to-two-week time horizon are characterized by a very high level of detail in terms of the number of activities pertaining to each task and in the completeness of their specifications. Action Plans focus on limited areas within the project that are usually the responsibility of low-level supervisors. Delegating action planning to those who are closer to the work enhances ownership and commitment to the plan and distributes the planning effort more evenly among management levels.

Being at the hub of internal and external project information (as will be discussed in the next chapter), the project manager is in the best position to lead the periodic updating of the medium-term plans. Such Look-Ahead Plans' time horizons typically vary from two to six months. By preparing and studying the implications of such a tentative plan early on, the project manager is able to ensure the effectiveness of subsequent Action Plans.

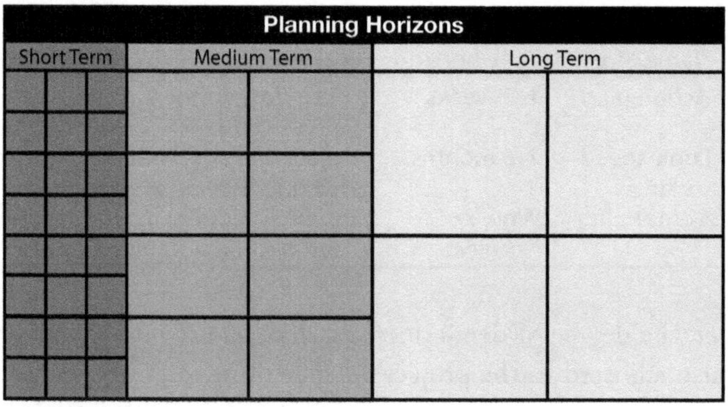

Planning Horizons		
Short Term	Medium Term	Long Term

Fig. 2.2   Influence of planning horizon on degree of detail

It should be stressed that project managers don't make many of the planning decisions on their own because of time constraints and because they often lack the technical expertise. Still, project managers play a major role in the decision-making process: They facilitate deliberations, they link members of the team to the appropriate stakeholders, they frame decisions (e.g., by developing the criteria for decision making), they set the pace of the decision-making process, and most importantly, they ensure that the multiple interdependent decisions and plans are well integrated.

Preparing and presenting the Master Plan requires more formal and sophisticated procedures than those required for the Action Plan and the Look-Ahead Plan, and it is usually led by the project scheduler. While the only way for coping with missing and changing information is to establish long-term flexibility, the Master Plan usually includes redundancies and backup systems, thus ensuring external parties that major project milestones and objectives will be met. Redundancies are discussed later in this chapter [12, 13]. (See Table 2.1 for a summary of the Rolling Wave plans.)

This style of planning does not imply that decisions should be arbitrarily "put off until later." Rather, it is an act of deliberately splitting off those planning aspects that can be acted upon more opportunely in the future. By applying this approach, two extreme situations are avoided. The first is the preparation of overly detailed plans too soon, which may lead to rapid obsolescence because some decisions are based on information provided by intelligent guesses rather than on reliable data. The other extreme situation is delaying the planning until all the information is complete and stable. In both cases, project effectiveness will suffer. One can make timely and firm decisions only by adopting the planning style that provides greater detail at the appropriate stage of the project.

Table 2.1 The various plans that go into a "rolling wave" approach

Goals	Name of plan	Time horizon	Created by
Short term	Action plan	1–2 weeks	Those close to the work
Mid term	Look ahead plan	2–6 months	Project manager, resulting from decision-making process
Long term	Master plan	Whole of project	Project scheduler; includes redundancies and backup systems

However, the degree of detail does not depend only on the planning horizon; it is also adjusted to the project's degree of uncertainty. The plan should provide a correspondingly higher degree of detail if uncertainty is low. When uncertainty is high, the formal plan's degree of detail for the near term is reduced and its decrease is accelerated across the planning horizon.

The frequency of updating the plans is also contingent upon uncertainty; that is, the greater the uncertainty, the greater the frequency of planning revisions. In a study that focused on a $20-million project lasting 18 months, major revisions that included changes in implementation methods or changes in the sequence of activities were found to be introduced on an average of every 3.5 months. Under conditions of high uncertainty, frequency of updating was estimated to increase to an average of every 1.5 months [14].

Develop a Learning-Based Project Planning and Control Process

The first project manager of JASSM (the Joint Air-to-Surface Standoff Missile project of the US Air Force) required that all members of the team keep meticulous schedules of their daily activities. With these firm instructions being continuously monitored, Brian Rutledge, the financial manager of the project, soon found himself spending more time documenting his activities than doing actual work. One Friday at a 6 p.m. meeting when the team discussed the upcoming visit of representatives from five companies scheduled for the following week, someone put up his schedule for next week on the overhead. It included a line that read "Drive to the bakery, pick up donuts." The deputy project manager commented that this was exactly what he wanted to see in the schedules of each member of the team. Brian Rutledge was not surprised when that project manager was unable to make meaningful progress and was replaced several months later.

Project Control

One of the classic roles of project planning is to facilitate project control. If planning establishes the targets and the course to reach them, control is the process that ensures the course of action is maintained and desired targets are reached. Control involves not only measuring and evaluating performance but also taking corrective action when performance diverges from plans.

Unfortunately, the commonly held belief that better "control" is achieved when the plans are very detailed often leads the customer to require overly detailed and comprehensive Master Plans. Contractors must comply and are forced to go through the ritual of applying sophisticated tools to produce cumbersome plans in the form of scheduling networks. Marketed as symbols of managerial professionalism and the key to project success, these unmanageable and cluttered plans are in fact more likely to obscure the overview of the project.

One key difference between the traditional planning approach (in which both short- and long-term plans are prepared in advance at great detail) and the successful application of the rolling wave approach becomes evident during project control, when implementation deviates from the plan. In the traditional planning approach, the project team attempts to answer the question: Why didn't our performance yesterday conform to the original plan? In the rolling wave approach, project managers add another question: What can we learn from the performance data to improve the next cycle of planning? In other words, they attempt to learn from their mistakes [15].

Cultural Change

» Effective learning from mistakes will happen only if the people who are actually doing the work are not micromanaged

---

For learning to take place during project control, a cultural change is required. Effective learning from mistakes will happen only if the people who are actually doing the work are not micromanaged. Rather, their work environment must encourage them to propose changes to the various project plans and to openly reveal and discuss their mistakes.

Ray Morgan, the project manager of Pathfinder, a solar-powered airplane, created a totally different planning culture within his team. He wished to use the schedule as a means not only for communicating the overall picture of what needed to be done, when and why, but also for actively engaging the entire team in updating and using their schedule. He, therefore, put a graphic depiction of the schedule on the side of a large container right in the hangar, next to the flight test crew and the airplane. The team was encouraged not to simply adhere to the original plan but to add and delete tasks interactively. These changes were incorporated into a computer model and were reprinted once or twice a week during flight tests. The team often referred back to the chart to help redefine the importance of a current task and to see how it fit into "the big picture." Thus, the schedule resulting from the ongoing learning was owned by the team.

Project Reviews

》Too often, the schedule of the project is owned not by the team but by the client and upper management

---

Too often, the schedule of the project is owned not by the team but by the client and upper management. The same problem exists in the ongoing assessment, which frequently comes in the form of project reviews. Brian Muirhead from NASA, who led the design, development, and launch of the flight system for the Pathfinder mission to Mars, describes the prevailing atmosphere during the review process:

> The routine is daunting. Members of the board sit at a horseshoe-shaped table, the chairman in the middle. A team member stands in front of them and launches his presentation. It usually isn't long before one of the review board members interrupts the presenter with a question—rather like an attorney presenting oral arguments before the Supreme Court. The skeptical expressions, the intense looks, the scowls and smiles are giveaways. And just as at the Supreme Court, the questions are generally polite, occasionally harsh, but all with a clear aim of probing for the truth [16].

Probing, but for the needs of upper management. Too often during such project reviews, insufficient attention is paid to the overall needs of the project team, and in particular to the negative implications of the preparations required for the review. Brian Muirhead discusses the time leading up to a project review during the Pathfinder mission:

> Formal project reviews come with a clear, but unavoidable, downside. Done well, the preparations can take an enormous amount of time for the team. Preparations for a formal board review can take too many of us—me and the project's top managers plus a number of key managers and engineers at the next level down—off the line for as much as six weeks. Necessary to the overall process, but a significant distraction; and even worse, a significant loss in momentum [17].

Two other project managers at NASA, dissatisfied with the time-consuming review process and its total focus on control, which benefits primarily the reviewer rather than the persons being reviewed, took steps to radically change the process.

Following a review session in the midst of a project at NASA's Goddard Space Flight Center, Marty Davis was a frustrated project manager. The existing review process may have fulfilled upper management's need to control its operations, but Marty Davis felt it did not fulfill his team's need to learn from the reviewers how to cope better with their major challenges. Therefore, he modified the process to give his team the best input for identifying problems and the best advice for solving them. This meant doing away with the usual "trial court" atmosphere at NASA review sessions. In its place, Marty Davis developed a review process that provided feedback from independent, supportive experts and encouraged joint problem solving.

The first thing Marty Davis did was to unilaterally specify the composition of the review panel to fit the unique needs of his project, making sure that the panel members agreed with his concept of an effective review process. The second thing he did was change the structure of the sessions, devoting the first day to his team's presentations and the second day to one-on-one, in-depth discussions between the panel and the team members to come up with possible solutions to the problems identified on the first day. This modified process enabled Marty Davis to create a working climate based on trust and respect, in which his team members could safely share their doubts and concerns. The independent experts identified areas of concern, many of which, after one-on-one meetings with the specialized project staff and the review team's technical specialists, were resolved. The issues that remained open were assigned a Request for Action (RFA). Eventually, Marty Davis was left with just five RFAs.

» learning-based reviews are a must

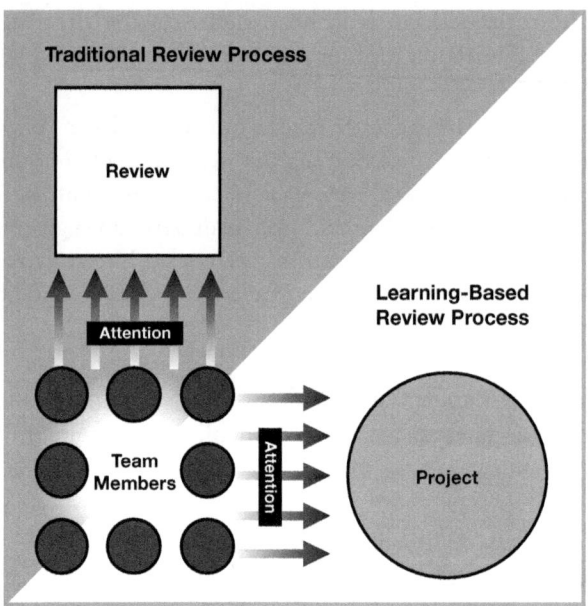

Fig. 2.3 In the traditional review process, team members expend their energy on the review rather than the project. In a learning-based review, team members focus on communicating the status of their work for the purpose of troubleshooting

Susan Motil, another project manager from NASA, used Marty Davis's model after a bad experience with Concept Review. Susan Motil compared the direct outcomes of the initial, unsuccessful Concept Review and the second review based on Marty Davis's model. The latter model allowed the team to spend significantly less time and effort on the RFAs, and it cost the project about $200,000, as compared to the $700,000 price tag for the initial review [15, 18–20]. Both Marty Davis and Susan Motil concluded that learning-based reviews are a must. They can help identify problems in your project, which may make the difference between mission failure and mission success, and if implemented effectively, they can be accomplished without excessive interruption to project progress and with limited extra cost (Fig 2.3).

Successful managers of more traditional projects, such as designing and building manufacturing facilities, also practice learning-based project reviews. P&G has replaced review panels comprised of external experts or senior managers with peer-review panels. These panels last four to eight hours and follow a simple protocol: First, the project team concisely communicates its technical and execution strategies, and then the floor is opened to all the invited peers for comments, critiques, and clarifying questions. Out of the numerous notes documented throughout the review process, 5 to 10 "nuggets" usually emerge that the project team uses to improve the technical, cost, and scheduling aspects of the project. Sometimes, the invited peers even take one or two of the "nuggets" back to their own projects [21].

Maintain Stability by Adding an Appropriate Amount of Redundancy

Planning generally strives for using resources efficiently. That is, upon completion of a project, ideally, no unused resources remain. There are times, however, when successful project managers can better maintain stable plans by carefully adding slack resources. In the following example, Bill Clegern, a project manager from Procter & Gamble, faced a dilemma which is common in project life: Should one risk being shorthanded but efficient, or should one eliminate the risk by adding a backup system?

As part of construction site preparation, the existing plant's firefighting water tank needed to be relocated 100 yards across the site. No risks for lost production could be tolerated. Since there was no other reliable source of water, the tank had to be moved, reconnected, tested, and started up during a long weekend, when production was down.

The basic scheme was to use two 50-ton cranes to pick up and walk the tank across a newly cleared pathway covered by a bed of compacted limestone gravel. The contractor's construction manager was absolutely sure the plan would work. Every disaster scenario was discussed by the team and worked through with an ultimate positive outcome—until the possibility of a crane breakdown was raised.

The possibility was remote, and the contractor felt that he could repair any normal failure in the field or, in the worst-case scenario, get parts or call in another crane. However, Bill Clegern, the project manager, assumed that breakdowns do happen and did not want to be in a position of failing because of an "act of God." He made the decision to bring in a standby crane, taking full responsibility for "squandering money" on a seemingly redundant piece of equipment. Things went smoothly until one of the active cranes blew a 2-inch hydraulic hose. The backup was brought in and the job went on. The contractor found that he could not in fact repair the hose on site and acknowledged that Bill Clegern's initial decision to arrange for a backup was what allowed them to stay on schedule. He had learned his lesson and immediately sent his buyer to work telephoning around to rent another backup.

But then, to top things off, it started to rain! Sewers throughout the city backed up, roads became flooded, and the people at the site were blocked from leaving. That would have been tragic enough if a crane or hose had been available, but neither were! The long weekend had attracted a lot of outage work, tying up every sizable crane in the area. No hose was available either. Luckily, no further disasters or unplanned events occurred; the plant started up as scheduled. In retrospect, the contractor's construction manager regretted not planning for the rain. If he'd prepared the pathway with swales to form a dike, he was sure he could have floated the tank into place. No cranes would have been necessary [22].

Risk Analysis

Why didn't Bill Clegern make his choice based on quantitative risk analysis? [23, 24] While a lot has been written on risk management, there is ample evidence that it is rarely employed in today's projects and its effectiveness is questionable. Zur Shapira, who asked several hundred top executives (of permanent organizations, not of projects) what they thought about risk management, found they had little use for probabilities of different outcomes. They also did not find much relevance in the calculate-and-decide paradigm. Probability estimates were just too abstract for them. As for projects, which are temporary and unique endeavors, it is usually not possible to accumulate sufficient historical data to develop reliable probabilities, even when the risky situation can be clearly defined [25].

Indeed, weaknesses similar to those described by Zur Shapira are reported regarding risk treatment in projects. Brian Muirhead from NASA disclosed that when his team members were asked to estimate the probability of failures, "Many people simplistically assign numbers to this analysis—implying a degree of accuracy that has no connection with reality" [26]. Flyvbjerg et al. reported that risk management is not a common practice, even in very large projects, which are known to suffer from significant cost overruns: "In a World Bank study of 92 projects, only a handful was found to contain 'thoughtful' risk analyses showing 'good practice'" [27].

❯❯we should give up the delusion of managing risk

In his recent analysis "The Risks of Risk Management," Gary Klein, a highly recognized authority on the subject, concluded unequivocally, "In complex situations, we should give up the delusion of managing risk.

We cannot foresee or identify risks, and we cannot manage what we can't see or understand" [28]. It therefore behooves us to build in some redundancies so that we're able to cope with problems that may arise.

Klein calls such an active approach "anticipate and adapt," which we'll discuss in Chap. 4 as part of the "resilience engineering" discipline.

Decision Choreographer: The First Role of the Project Manager

Planning is a decision-making process requiring the integration of interdependent decisions. The decisions made throughout the project lifespan may relate to

- Different *stages* of the project, including the feasibility/conceptual, definition, execution, and closeout stages.
- Different *functional aspects* of the project, such as cost, time, quality, human resources, engineering, and procurement.
- Different *participants*, such as upper management, clients, end users, designers, contractors, suppliers, and core team members.
- Different time horizons, that is, short-, medium-, and long-term horizons.

In today's projects, which have to cope with a dynamic environment and frequent changes in project requirements, methods of execution, and participating parties, and which may require regular updating and revising of decisions, integrating decisions is an extremely dynamic and complex task.

The project managers are responsible for coordinating and integrating the multiple decisions made by the various parties at different stages of the project, to ensure coherent and timely plans. In this role, the project manager performs very much like a dance choreographer whose role is to move and synchronize the dancers—decisions—to create a harmonious dance—an integrated plan (Fig. 2.4).

Key Points

- Project objectives should not be finalized too early; they are contingent on some of the early outcomes of the project.
- It may be wise to bring contractors in on the objective formulation and to create prototypes to aid in objective formulation.

Fig. 2.4 The project manager performs very much like a dance choreographer whose role is to move and synchronize the dancers—decisions—to create a harmonious dance—an integrated plan

- The rolling wave approach incorporates plans of varying detail and time horizons.
- In the rolling wave approach, project managers ask, "What can we learn from the performance data to improve the next cycle of planning?"
- Learning-based reviews can help identify problems in your project, and they can be accomplished without excessive interruption to project progress and with limited extra cost.

- Quantitative risk management is of questionable use; building in redundancies helps project managers cope with problems that may arise.
- The first role of the project manager is as a decision choreographer, who moves and synchronizes decisions to create an integrated plan.

References

1. Klein, G. *Streetlights and Shadows: Searching for the Keys to Adaptive Decision Making.* 2009, Cambridge, MA: MIT Press: p. 207.
2. Collins, M. Lessons from NASA Project Managers. *Ask Magazine* 2001; 3(June): p. 26–9.
3. Baker, N. R., Green, S. G., and Bean, A. S. Why Research and Development Projects Succeed or Fail. *Research Management* 1986; 29(6): p. 29–34.
4. Hauschildt, J., Goals and Problem-Solving in Innovative Decisions, in *Empirical Research on Organizational Decision-Making*, E. Witte, and H. J. Zimmermann, Editors. 1986, North-Holland: Elsevier: p. 3–19.
5. Laufer, A. Essentials of Project Planning: Owner's Perspective. *Journal of Management Engineering* 1990; 6(2): p. 162–176.
6. March, J. G., *The Technology of Foolishness, in Ambiguity and Choice in Organizations*, J. G. March, J. P. Olsen, S. Christensen, and M. D. Cohen, Editors. 1976, Bergen: Universitetsforlaget: p. 69–81.
7. Mintzberg, H. The Design School: Reconsidering the Basic Premises of Strategic Management. *Strategic Management Journal* 1990; 11(3): p. 171–195.
8. Engwall, M., *The Futile Dream of the Perfect Goal*, in *Beyond Project Management: New Perspectives on the Temporary-Permanent Dilemma*, K. Sahlin-Andersson and A. Soderholm, Editors. 2002, Stockholm Lund: Copenhagen Business School Press: p. 241–60.
9. Laufer, A., Post, T., and Hoffman, E. J. *Shared Voyage: Learning and Unlearning from Remarkable Projects.* 2005, Washington, DC: The NASA History Series.
10. Schrage, M. *Serious Play: How the World's Best Companies Simulate to Innovate.* 2000, Boston, MA: Harvard Business Press.
11. Laufer, A. *Simultaneous Management: Managing Projects in a Dynamic Environment.* 1997, New York, NY: AMACOM, American Management Association: p. 57–8.
12. Laufer, A. *Breaking the Code of Project Management.* 2009, New York, NY: Palgrave Macmillan: p. 46–48.
13. Smith, P. G. *Flexible Product Development: Building Agility for Changing Markets.* 2007, San Francisco, CA: Jossey-Bass: p. 186–8.
14. Cohenca, D., Laufer, A., and Ledbetter, W. B. Factors Affecting Construction Planning Efforts. *Construction Engineering and Management*, ASCE, 1989; 115(1): p. 70–89.

15. Edmondson, A. C. The Competitive Imperative of Learning. *Harvard Business Review* 2008; 86(7/8): p. 60–7.
16. Muirhead, B. and Simon, W. L. *High Velocity Leadership: The Mars Pathfinder Approach to Faster, Better, Cheaper.* 1999, New York, NY: Harper Business: p. 23–4.
17. Muirhead, B. and Simon, W. L. *High Velocity Leadership: The Mars Pathfinder Approach to Faster, Better, Cheaper.* 1999, New York, NY: Harper Business: p. 86–7.
18. Davis, M. Tangled Up in Reviews. *Ask Magazine* 2001; 4(July): p. 8–11.
19. Motil, S. So This Is Knowledge Sharing. *Ask Magazine* 2003; 10(January): p. 6–9.
20. Rice, M. P., O'Connor, G. C. O., and Pierantozzi, R. Implementing a Learning Plan to Counter Project Uncertainty. *MIT Sloan Management Review* 2008; 49(2): p. 19–22.
21. Cameron, S. The Hour Glass and the Project Manager. *Ask Magazine* 2001; 4(July): p. 27–8.
22. Laufer, A. *Simultaneous Management: Managing Projects in a Dynamic Environment.* 1997, New York, NY: AMACOM, American Management Association: p. 76–7.
23. *A Guide to the Project Management Body of Knowledge (PMBOK Guide)*, 3rd Ed., 2004, Newtown Square, Pennsylvania: Project Management Institute: p. 237–254.
24. *NASA Systems Engineering Handbook*, SP-6105, 1995, NASA: p. 37–44.
25. Shapira, Z. *Risk Taking: A Managerial Perspective.* 1995, New York, NY: Russell Sage Foundation: p. 21,43.
26. Muirhead, B. and Simon, W. L. *High Velocity Leadership: The Mars Pathfinder Approach to Faster, Better, Cheaper.* 1999, New York, NY: Harper Business: p. 37–8.
27. Flyvbjerg, B., Bruzelius, N., and Rothengatter, W. *Megaprojects and Risk: An Anatomy of Ambition.* 2003, Cambridge, UK: Cambridge University Press: p. 76.
28. Klein, G. *Streetlights and Shadows: Searching for the Keys to Adaptive Decision Making.* 2009, Cambridge, MA: MIT Press: p. 246–9.

3

The Agility Practice: Be Responsive and Action Oriented

"It is not the strongest of the species that survives, nor the most intelligent, but the one most responsive to change."
Charles Darwin

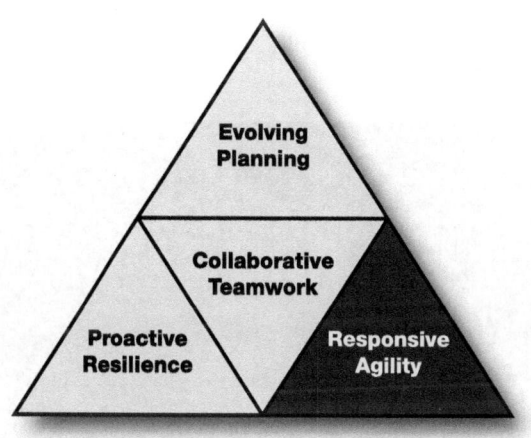

» agility: quick *action during* the execution phase

© The Author(s) 2018
A. Laufer et al., *Becoming a Project Leader*,
https://doi.org/10.1007/978-3-319-66724-9_3

Chapter 2 described how successful project managers cope with changes via cycles of planning, control, and ongoing learning. These practices are based on formal processes, where *decisions* are made *prior* to the next cycle of execution. However, in today's dynamic environment, projects must also cope with changes which require agility: quick action during the execution phase.

During the last decade many researchers have stressed that the project manager's key challenge today is coping with frequent unexpected events. Jim Wink, US Navy Lieutenant Commander, for example, reported that his team had encountered over 200 unexpected events during the life of a schedule-driven project [1]. The sources of such events may vary from one case to the next, with design errors, the failure of a contractor to show up, the bankruptcy of a supplier, and changes in the customers' specifications being common examples [2–12].

In her book *Plans and Situated Actions: The Problem of Human-Machine Communication*, Lucy Suchman describes two fundamentally different approaches to coping with unexpected events, drawing an analogy to the different methods employed by European and Trukese (Micronesian) navigators (Fig. 3.1).

> The European navigator begins with a plan—a course—which he has charted according to certain universal principles, and he carries out his voyage by relat-

Fig. 3.1 The Trukese Navigator steers according to the information provided by the wind, the tide, the stars, the clouds, and the sound of the water on the side of his boat

ing his every move to that plan. His effort throughout his voyage is directed to remaining "on course." If unexpected events occur, he must first alter the plan, then respond accordingly.

[The Trukese navigator] begins with an objective rather than a plan. He sets off towards the objective and responds to conditions as they arise in an ad hoc fashion. [And he] steers according to the information provided by the wind, the tide, the stars, the clouds, and the sound of the water on the side of his boat. While his objective is clear from the outset, his actual course is contingent on the unique circumstances that he cannot anticipate in advance. … His effort is directed to doing whatever is necessary to reach the objective. If asked, he can point to his objective at any moment, but he cannot describe his course. [13]

We have found in our research that successful project managers adopt both approaches, depending on the kind of changes they have to cope with. When the need to cope with a change becomes evident during the various planning and review iterations (weekly, monthly, or quarterly) described in Chap. 2, the project manager adopts the approach used by the European navigator. But changes discovered during the ongoing execution of a project may quickly become acute problems, and these very often require immediate action without referring back to the project plan.

The present chapter presents three guidelines commonly practiced among successful managers to address problems uncovered during project execution:

- Disseminate information frequently and routinely
- Respond and act with agility
- Manage by moving about and by enabling

Disseminate Information Frequently and Routinely

Fredrick Brooks, best known as the "father of the IBM System/360," argued that "the project manager's chief daily task is communication, not decision-making" [14]. Following a detailed study, Henry Mintzberg concluded that executives serve as the nerve center of their organizations by being constantly engaged in both receiving and disseminating information. In today's dynamic project environment, disseminating information frequently and routinely has become even more crucial for project success. It serves as a key practice for the early identification of unexpected events and for coping with them effectively [15, 16].

Frequent Person-to-Person Contact

Hugh Woodward, a project manager from Procter & Gamble, reached a similar conclusion through trial and error. His assignment was to secure an environmental permit for a new product. While several groups of people distributed over a wide geographic area were involved in the project, the product was fairly routine, the participants involved in the task had some experience working with each other, and the responsibility of each participant was clarified in a preliminary planning meeting which generated a detailed list of action steps and responsibilities. No hitches were expected.

Yet the schedule was slipping continually. A second planning process was initiated with all involved parties, which resulted in a revised plan. Action steps, responsibilities, and deadlines were drawn. Assurances were given that the process flowsheet was now stable and that the formulated strategy for approaching the State regulators was valid.

Yet within days the schedule was slipping again! Hugh found that people were increasingly calling him to ask what do next. He realized that there was no forum which enabled the participants to communicate with each other. He thus initiated weekly video conferences with all the key participants meeting to share the latest information and to assess the project's status.

Through these weekly virtual meetings, the team members were able to quickly collect missing information, identify changes, and solve problems as they were still emerging—when finding solutions is easier and faster. Moreover, discussing unclear information openly and frequently reduced information ambiguity, eliminating the need for many of the changes they encountered prior to the weekly conference calls. It turned out that these weekly video conferences were all that was needed to assure the smooth progress of the project [17].

The concept of frequent communication is also at the center of the Agile methods for software development. In their book *Balancing Agility and Discipline: A Guide to the Perplexed*, Boehm and Turner compared communication in the typical plan-driven methods and in the Agile methods: "Plan-driven methods rely heavily on documented process plans (schedules, milestones, procedures) and product plans (requirements, architecture, standards) to keep everyone coordinated. … Agile methods generally rely on more frequent, person-to-person communication" [18].

In their classic book *Implementation*, Majone and Wildavsky argued that planning alone could not guarantee the elimination of unexpected events: "The planning model recognizes that implementation may fail because the original plan was infeasible. But it does not recognize the important point that many, perhaps most, constraints remain hidden in the planning stage, and are only discovered in the implementation process" [19].

Daily Updates

To cope with the late discovery of hidden constraints and changes, successful project managers update their teams daily. NASA's Tony Schoenfelder described some of the communication practices employed by John Hodge, the first leader of the Space Station Task Force:

> Hodge combined a number of practices and innovations that led to a unique and uninhibited atmosphere. Each day started at 8:15 AM with an unstructured 15-minute all-hands stand-up meeting. Only those who had something important to say took the floor, while everyone else crowded into the office or hallway to listen. It turned out to be a useful device in that it not only conveyed information, but also physically reunited the team each morning to reinforce the spirit of camaraderie and the sense of shared purpose. ... Hodge didn't believe in secrets. He was completely open with the staff. What he knew, they knew. Members appreciated this unusual candor and reciprocated by keeping him and the leadership well informed. ... Hodge was liable to pop up unannounced anywhere at anytime. ... He not only got to know each person as a person, but also received an unfiltered heads-up as to what was going on. [20]

Matt Peterson, at the Boldt Construction Company, used a similar practice. All on-site team members (the superintendent, field engineers, project coordinator, safety officer, etc.) participated in "daily 10-minute huddles." Matt reported that these informal morning meetings not only ensured that the team members understood one another's current workloads and constraints but often enabled them to identify and resolve conflicting priorities before they became problems [21].

» Insufficient updated information from the client is one of the more prevalent causes for unexpected changes

---

Insufficient updated information from the client is one of the more prevalent causes for unexpected changes. Yet, project managers tend to communicate with their clients primarily at the early stages of the project, while the project's requirements are first formulated, and subsequent communication is often saved for crisis moments. Don Margolies, a NASA project manager based in Maryland, explained why and how he communicated with his client, Dr. Edward Stone, who served as the head of the science team and was based in California:

Dr. Stone and I set up a schedule to talk with each other on the phone every week. In the early stages of the project, much of what was about to unfold was still up in the air. You might say the spacecraft itself was about the only thing not in the air. I thought it was crucial to the success of the project that Dr. Stone know everything that was going on—and if something happened that involved the development of the instruments, he could be on it right away. Even if it was just to say that the weather was nice in California and there was nothing much happening here at Goddard, we always kept our phone appointment. [22]

Thus, Don communicated with his client not only in time of crisis but routinely throughout the life of the project. He reported that the benefits of these routine and brief weekly phone calls became evident more than a few times during the project. Their ability, for example, to identify in advance possible cost overruns, enabled them ultimately to complete the $140 million project at $30 million under budget!

❯❯ disseminating information frequently and routinely contributes to both flexibility and stability

Importantly, disseminating information frequently and routinely contributes to both flexibility and stability. That is, the team's ability to adapt and solve problems as soon as they occur enables it to quickly regain stability. In Chap. 4, we will elaborate on how today's successful project managers strive to allow for both stability and flexibility [23, 24].

Respond and Act with Agility

While frequent communication has a vital role in identifying problems early, coping with unexpected events often demands quick action. Thus, project managers may need to use creative improvisations to quickly deal with such events. Brian Muirhead, who was responsible for the development and launch of the Mars Pathfinder flight system, had this to say:

"Everybody understands the need for a plan. … But in a world of Faster, Better, Cheaper, improvising should be seen as an inseparable part of planning, the other half of a complete process. Improvisations are characterized by there being no split between design and production, where thinking and doing unfold simultaneously. In the fast-paced, rapidly changing world in which we now live and do business, the ability to improvise has risen to the top of the priority list of managerial skills" [25–27].

Improvisation

In the following three examples, project managers employed improvisation to cope expediently with unexpected surprises. The first example is told by NASA's Kenneth Szalai, who served as the chief engineer and software manager for the first digital fly-by-wire aircraft:

> A systems engineer called me and told me that the preflight self-test had failed. … While troubleshooting, I froze and my heart sank. The problem was far worse than some self-test tolerance setting. I discovered that a half-dozen instructions did not match the program listing! … The flight computer had contaminated instructions. We did not have the means to automatically check the computer memory against the accurate printed listing. … The Draper Laboratory and IBM identified the cause of the problem the next day. An error in the "Assembler" software was found. … IBM started to fix the Assembler flaw. … [But] I estimated it would take them a couple of weeks, and we were supposed to fly next week. … I laughed to myself and thought: How long would it take to manually check the computer memory dump against the listing? Let's see, there are 25,000 memory locations, if we had five teams of engineers, and they could read aloud and verify one memory location every 10 seconds, five teams could verify 30 memory locations in a minute. That would take about 14 hours. … We got a few more than five teams together, alternated the reader and verifier every couple of pages or so, and added breaks. We finished by Friday afternoon and did not find any other errors. I guess sometimes pioneering work needs solutions rather than elegance. … We flew on Wednesday, as Carl had asked. [28]

Facing enormous time pressure, Kenneth came up with a spontaneous improvisation that provided a simple, albeit inelegant, solution to the problem.

Rex Geveden, a project manager at NASA, also resorted to some effective inelegance when he was informed that an instrument had failed its vibration test because a bracket wasn't strong enough. Fixing the problem in accordance with NASA's standard procedures, which involved redesigning, manufacturing, and inspecting the bracket, would have taken at least two weeks. Instead, Rex allowed his Chief Engineer, Fred Sanders, who had the knowledge and skills, to take over. Fred had their shop cut the pieces according to the sketches he had drawn. He then proceeded to take the bracket home, drill and tap it, fastening it to the panels. The repaired bracket was successfully tested the next day [29].

It seems that Rex's actions were endorsed by NASA since he was later promoted to the position of NASA's Chief Engineer and subsequently promoted to the prominent role of NASA's Associate Administrator.

Leslie Shepherd had to come up with a unique solution while managing a renovation project for the US federal government. Because the buildings were occupied at the time, the project manager was required to work around the tenants and the existing site conditions, and to do it quickly. They encountered a problem when the roof of a fully occupied office building was being covered with roofing tar as part of the renovation. The fumes from the tar were being pulled in by the building's fresh air intakes, making it impossible for the tenants to work. The building manager could have shut down the air intake system for a few hours at a time, but not for the entire day. After considering his options, Leslie decided to take a nontraditional approach to solving the problem.

> My solution may not have been elegant, but it was effective. We hired someone to stand on the roof next to the air intakes and sniff for tar fumes. The building manager trained the new worker how to turn the air intake fans on and off. He started work the very next day, turning the fans on or off, depending on his olfactory reflexes. That was his only job, and the additional salary for this "Official Sniffer" was far less than the lost hours resulting from interrupted work that had to be covered by the tenants. The building manager received no more complaints about the tar fumes for the entire duration of the roofing project. [30]

Leslie, like Kenneth and Rex, was under a great deal of time pressure. All three managers could quickly implement their solutions because of their simplicity, yet each of them employed a somewhat different approach. Kenneth's solution can be termed "bricolage" given that he applied a combination of the resources at hand to solve the pressing problem. The key to solving the problem for Rex involved adaptation—that is, adjusting the solution to the new conditions. As for Leslie, his success can simply be attributed to creativity [31, 32].

Agile Responses

Most unexpected events faced by today's project managers are not associated with the same extreme contexts and constraints as those described in the three previous examples; thus, they usually do not require significant improvisation. However, they do require fast, agile responses. During a three-year consulting work by this book's authors with 20 very successful project managers at Boldt Construction Company, we watched them respond with agility and take immediate actions to cope with frequent unexpected events. Here are four brief examples:

Unlevel Floor

The blackout curtains to be installed in a large hospital were supposed to hang somewhere between 1/16" and 1/4" off the floor. In several rooms, the curtains were not meeting the requirement because the floor was not level. After discussing the problem with the project's carpenter, the project manager decided that the inconsistent curtain height could be compensated for using metal beaded chains and connectors. After receiving approval from the client, the project manager made a quick trip to the local retail store and purchased the parts needed to complete the fix. The issue was resolved in less than four hours.

Outdated Drawings

The steel supplier fabricated the support steel for some air-handling units using outdated drawings. The steel arrived on-site before the mistake was caught. The project manager was left with two choices: Send it back and have the supplier fix the mistake (at no cost), or have the team members fix it in the field. The project manager, along with his superintendent, decided that even though fixing the mistake on-site would cost the team a few hours of extra labor, it was preferable to waiting several days, until replacements arrived from the supplier.

Missing Information

The drawings of the equipment did not arrive when expected. The electrical contractor was threatening to stop all his underground rough-in until the information was received. Stopping all the work would have had a serious impact on the schedule. The team met on-site to review what information was still missing. Based on this information, the project manager decided to install junction boxes at the perimeter of the equipment rooms so that a majority of the work could continue, leaving the rooms to be roughed in at a later date.

New Sustainability Manager

The plumbing contractor was told to install 1.6 gallons-per-flush toilets in the building. After the original decision to use these toilets had been made, the owner hired a new sustainability manager, who wanted lower-flow toilets instead. There were concerns with the functionality of the lower-flow toilets, so

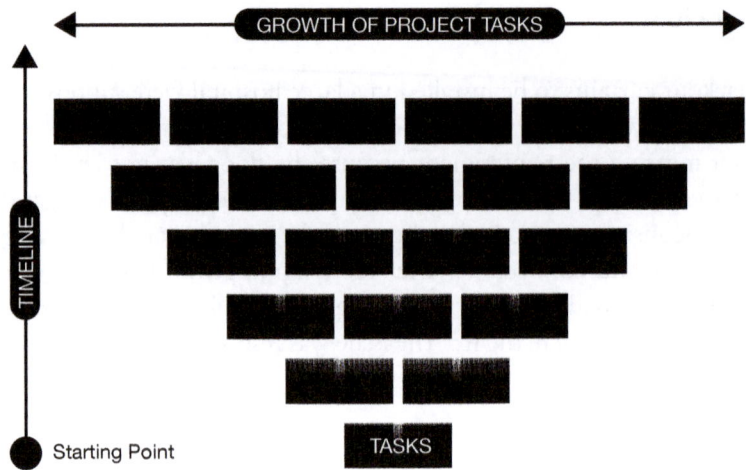

Fig. 3.2 Unexpected events affecting one task can have a domino effect on many subsequent interdependent tasks

the project manager recommended installing a mock-up of each type of toilet. After testing the mock-up, everyone was in agreement on the preferred fixture. Using the mock-up to resolve the concerns allowed them to avoid a schedule impact.

Interdependent Tasks

Why is it crucial to take fast action to resolve such problems? Due to the organizational structure of projects in which tasks are tightly interconnected, when unexpected events affect one task, many other *interdependent tasks* may also be quickly impacted (see Fig. 3.2). For example, affected contractors may decide to move their workforces to other projects, making it difficult to bring them back on time once the problem is resolved.

》 all the events that have the power to excite people and engage them in their work, the single most important is making progress

---

Thus, solving problems as soon as they emerge is vital for maintaining work progress, a conclusion drawn in 1971 by a pair of researchers at Columbia University. Sayles and Chandler studied project managers at NASA and found that they routinely strived to *maintain forward momentum*: "In working to maintain a forward momentum, the manager seeks to avoid stalemates. ... In a good many situations, corrective action is possible only during a brief 'window.' ... The heart of the matter is **quickness of response**" [33]. Similarly, Muirhead and Simon have concluded, "Maintaining momentum is a cornerstone of successful management ... more important than always being right" [25]. Interrupting project momentum may also have an indirect negative impact on the motivation and commitment of the workforce. In their book *The Progress Principle*, Amabile and Kramer argue that "of all the events that have the power to excite people and engage them in their work, the single most important is making progress" [34].

Successful project managers strive to minimize the severity and duration of the impact of unexpected events in order to regain project stability as soon as possible and restart work according to the project plans. They embrace the agile approach demonstrated by the Trukese navigator, but once the problems are solved, they prefer the planning approach of the European navigator. It should be also stressed that the rolling wave approach to project planning (described in Chap. 2) facilitates the agility practice; the action plans with their very short time horizon (a week or two) render project planning more agile. We will elaborate on the blending of planning and agility in the next chapter [35, 36].

» To be successful in practicing responsive agility, a project manager must operate within an organizational culture that acknowledges the unavoidability of unexpected events

---

To be successful in practicing responsive agility, a project manager must operate within an organizational culture that acknowledges the unavoidability of unexpected events. According to Steve Kerr, Chief Learning Officer of General Electric, "The future is moving so quickly that you can't anticipate it. ... We have put a tremendous emphasis on quick response. ... We will continue to be surprised, but we won't be surprised that we are surprised" [37]. Organizations would benefit from having a similar attitude. As Theodore Rubin, a past president of the American Institute for Psychoanalysis, wrote, "The problem is not that there are problems. The problem is expecting otherwise and thinking that having problems is a problem" [38].

Manage by Moving About and by Enabling

Moving about enables the project manager to accomplish the two previous guidelines, to disseminate information and to respond and act with agility. In their book *A Passion for Excellence*, Tom Peters and Nancy Austin write that "the number one productivity problem in America is, quite simply, managers who are out of touch with their people." Peters and Austin suggest that the best way for management to be in touch with people is to actually see them face-to-face. Thus, it is crucial for managers to leave the confines of an office and visit with team members at their workplace. In today's dynamic environment, plagued with unexpected events, such managerial mobility is even more important [39].

The Consequences of Remote Control

The following two stories exemplify what can happen when managers avoid moving about and think they can control performance from afar by requiring detailed reports. The first is a bizarre episode from the novel *Doctors* by Erich Segal:

> Barney Livingston was in his first week as an intern on Surgery, eager and proud to be in the operating room with the chief surgeon, Dr. Aubrey, and the anesthesiologist, Dr. Nagy, who were considered to be the top specialists in their fields. It was to be a routine removal of a gallbladder.
>
> It started out smoothly enough, but then the anesthesiologist reported problems. The patient's temperature soared to 108, the EKG started "going crazy," and then, when Dr. Aubrey felt for the femoral pulse, "Barney could tell from the expression above his mask that he had found none." The EKG was pronounced flat; Mr. A was dead. "There was a sudden flood of silence. No one dared speak until Dr. Aubrey decided on a course of action. At last he ordered, 'Dr. Nagy, continue aerating the lungs.'"
>
> "Barney watched in growing disbelief," unable to fathom why they started sewing him up. And then, when Dr. Aubrey ordered that Mr. A be taken to the recovery room, Barney was stunned. He turned to Dr. Aubrey's assistant and said, "Will you please explain to me why the hell you pumped air into a guy who's so dead he had no pulse or heartbeat?"
>
> The assistant explained that this way, "Mr. A would be pronounced dead after the operation by someone in the recovery room."
>
> "'You mean just for Aubrey's ego?' Barney replied with astonishment."
>
> "No," [the assistant] protested, "Tom's a bigger man than that. But you can't imagine how much paperwork he's saved—even though I usually do it for him. All the damn certificates, hospital papers, insurance forms—that bureaucratic crap takes hours. Now it'll be a job for the boys in post-op." [40]

Doctors may be a work of fiction, but Pfeffer and Sutton found that similar bizarre experiences are quite common in a wide variety of businesses: "In our field research, we encountered example after example of measurement processes that fueled destructive behavior inside organizations." Indeed, one can't ignore the vast body of empirical research on the frequency and magnitude of information-filtering and distortion within organizations [41–43].

» Remote control rarely offers real control

From a management-control point of view, the fundamental question is this: How can such a practice go unnoticed for such a long time that it becomes routine and the entire team naturally accepts it, with no hesitation or surprise? The answer is that *remote control rarely offers real control*. As Jerry Madden, a project manager at NASA, explains in the following story, real control comes from **mobility**:

> A highly-regarded vendor had large manufacturing contracts with NASA. Its manufacturing reports listed the items that had been delivered to us. After going through one lengthy report, I went down to the integration floor expecting to see an assembled spacecraft. I found that many assemblies that had been listed were missing.
>
> Jerry immediately called the vendor to report the errors and was told that they had two sets of paperwork: manufacturing reports for delivered items and integration returns for those items that were sent back for repairs or corrections. Once the item had been shipped back, the vendor closed out the manufacturing report.
>
> As Jerry realized, "It just goes to show that you can't rely on the official sources. If a project manager wants effective control, he/she has to always be on the move and ask questions. Indeed, 'things are seldom what they seem.'" [44]

Coaching

Managers who maintain a stationary position may be forced to make complex judgments with incomplete or misleading information. The "old school" approach to planning and control, which emphasizes control as a way of facilitating adherence to the plan, is much like using a thermostat to maintain a predetermined temperature. But in today's dynamic environment, a more suitable metaphor for project control would be coaching. A coach needs to see the game in order to guide the team and would hardly be effective if forced to coach from the locker room while receiving statistics via a monitor (Fig. 3.3).

Fig. 3.3 True project control comes from hands-on coaching, not armchair coaching

In the following story, Terry Little, a project manager with the US Air Force, describes how he applied Jerry's advice "to always be on the move and ask questions." Terry attempted to prevent problems before they happened—"to detect the smoke and thus eliminate the need to fight the fire."

I visited one of the contractors' suppliers and asked him, "What is the prime contractor making you do, or causing you to do, that you think is worthless or not value-added enough to offset the cost?" A representative from the prime contractor was present, and so there was a little bit of nervousness on the part of the supplier. I told the representative to go get a cup of coffee. I ended up with about three pages full of stuff that the supplier said was causing him headaches. As I was writing all this down, he asked, "What are you going to do with that?" And I said, "Not to worry."

How did I gain his trust? Well, for one thing, I was there. A government program manager does not normally go to visit the suppliers of a prime contractor. The fact that I was there and willing to spend a whole day looking at his facility, meeting his people, and talking to them about the program and how important their contributions were—that was a big deal to him.

Typically, the government says, "Our contract is with the prime, and we don't have a contract with these suppliers." [But] a large part of the success of the program depends on what the suppliers to my contractor are doing, [so] I believe it's important to communicate with everybody that's involved in the outcome of a program.

I gave the three pages to the prime without any explanation other than, "This is what he told me." A week later, this guy from the prime came back to me and explained how they'd addressed everything on the list except for one thing, and he gave me a detailed and satisfactory explanation as to why the one thing was still important to do. [45]

❯❯To ensure that moving about results in essential learning rather than destructive micromanagement, it must be accompanied by mutual trust

Terry took pains to gain the trust of his suppliers because merely "moving about" does not guarantee that the information collected will be reliable. Indeed, when subordinates or suppliers perceive managers as "corporate policemen," they develop tactics to conceal or distort information, much like Dr. Aubrey in the excerpt from *Doctor*. To ensure that moving about results in essential learning rather than destructive micromanagement, it must be accompanied by mutual trust.

Moving about helps foster the project manager's image as one who is not detached from the actual work and workers, but who is instead well informed, both with respect to the big picture and to the small details. This image, coupled with the respect and credibility gained, may help the project manager influence not only the work (by quickly solving specific problems) but the workers themselves.

Enabling

Unfortunately, moving about may not be sufficient in today's project environment. As described in the following two stories, today's successful project managers must also focus on *enabling* their project teams to better cope with the constant stream of unexpected events and problems. The first story is told by Karen Dorsey at Skanska, who participated in a one-year leadership development program we led at the company. At the time we interviewed her, she was the assistant project manager of a large construction project in New York City.

One-hundred eighty million dollars was allocated to repowering the Con Ed East River, a steam export plant that provides steam to all of lower Manhattan, including Wall Street and the financial district. When Skanska bid for and won the project, it was fraught with problems. Just to name a few: The original designer was terminated before design was complete, the owner did not want to pay a design engineer for coordination drawings, and the equipment design was based on original design drawings which resulted in multiple significant unexpected conflicts in the field.

Furthermore, since the East River project had been delayed several times, by the time the new plans came out, Skanska was already working on a different power project, and their key personnel were elsewhere engaged. The new project manager (Don) hired for the project was not yet available to start until about a month after the site had been mobilized. Once he arrived, it took a while for him to get up to speed.

Due to the multiple design issues and frequent changes from the client, no less than 1500 Requests for Information were submitted during the course of the project! Work could not be planned properly, and productivity was very low. The project was thus behind schedule, over budget, and had a bad safety rating. It was clear to all that the project was set up to fail. [46]

But, as recalled by Karen, things panned out differently:

Our new project manager, Don, was a very experienced, competent, and hard-working person, but most importantly, he was the ultimate enabler. To enable us to do our work with minimal distractions from the client and upper management, Don managed both, drastically reducing the flow of changes and unexpected events.

But most of his time was devoted to direct involvement with the team. He kept the team focused on what was really important, helping us prioritize our efforts. At the same time, Don enabled us to do our jobs by empowering us to make decisions by ourselves regarding problematic issues and to take responsibility for executing them. His trust in our capabilities and his total commitment to the project and to the team, made us want to be better and do better.

I learned a lot from Don, but the one thing I really try to emulate is that we need to put our egos aside for the good of the project and the team. Don was very driven and highly committed, but it was never about him, it was always about project results and the team. As a result, we all felt we had a stake in the success of the project. [46]

We became an enthusiastic project team that worked hard during the day and then would go out together as a group after work to blow off some steam. Everyone was willing to pitch in and help. When it came time for outage work and we needed to have supervision on site around the clock, everyone pitched in, even if it meant missing the Super Bowl or a Memorial Day barbeque with family.

At the end of the day, the project was a great success, and we developed a strong relationship with the client that has served us well on other projects since then.

Terry Little, a project manager for the US Air Force, had a similarly galvanizing effect when he was abruptly instructed to leave his current project to head the Joint Air-to-Surface Standoff Missile (JASSM) project:

It was an ongoing, extremely challenging project, which after nine months of work showed very little progress. The first day on the job, Terry called a meeting with the 20 people who had been on the team with the recently fired project manager, who was well liked. As if switching project managers mid-course was not enough of a shock to the group, Terry told the group that the contractual documents for the five competing companies needed to be ready within six months. The team did not mince words telling Terry he had no idea what he was talking about! Terry stopped them in mid-sentence, restating that they had to figure out how to work together to make this happen within six months or the project would be cancelled.

Terry then explained to the team what he expected of them and what they should expect of him: "First, you need to put aside all of your paradigms and all of your ideas about how exactly we are going to do this and start with one basic assumption—that it's going to be done in six months. … I am counting on you. I am empowering you, as a group, to go figure out how to do this. My job is to facilitate things, to do whatever's necessary to make the bureaucracy move out of our way, so that it parts like the Red Sea parted for Moses—that's my job."

Lynda Rutledge, the project's systems engineer, provided examples of Terry's managerial approach. The Single Acquisition Management Plan (SAMP) was the basic document laying out how the program would be managed; it would be signed off on by the Pentagon. Generally, project managers farmed it out to their respective leads. Consequently, SAMPs rarely provided a comprehensive picture of how the parts fit together. In all her years as a systems engineer, Lynda had never heard of a project manager actually writing the SAMPs. What left a lasting impression on her was that Terry took the SAMP provided by the previous project manager, closed his office door, and disappeared for five days to rewrite the project plan. At the same time he did not shut everyone out.

As she recalled, "Occasionally, he would pop out of his office and show up at people's desks and ask something like 'How many targets do we have?' He would roll that answer in his head a few moments and then ask a few more questions. Eventually, he would return to his office and start typing again."

By the end of this process, he had re-rewritten approximately 90% of the original draft and cut its size down by more than half. [47]

But Terry's direct involvement and immediate problem-solving was only one facet of his effective managerial style. In Lynda's mind, the most important thing Terry did, after setting the contract goal, was stating, "I'm going to trust you guys to do the right thing to meet our goal, and I'll back up whatever you decide to do." What this meant was that while his expectations were very high, his trust and confidence in the team were equally high. Lynda did not have to worry anymore that the project manager would overrule her recommendations and decisions every time one of the companies complained, which allowed her to execute what she believed needed to be done. In his book *Managing*, Henry Mintzberg explains, "In the leading role, managers help bring out the energy that exists naturally within people." Mintzberg elaborates through the following quote of a prominent CEO: "It's not [the manager's] job to supervise or to motivate, but to liberate and to enable." [48] According to Lynda, this was exactly Terry's approach. He energized his team by liberating and enabling them.

Terry explained how the team wrestled with the problems after listening to him and working with him for a couple of weeks:

> The result was that problems didn't remain unsolved for long. People no longer scratched their heads and asked one another, "How should we make the right decision?" Now, there was a level of commitment that meant any problem had to be attacked with a sledgehammer. The team addressed all problems, no matter whose area it was in. They wouldn't let any given problem cause the rest of the team to fail. When a problem was detected, everybody marshaled their energies to quickly decide how to move forward, how to either solve the problem or get around it.
>
> Even after they got to the point where it became fairly certain that they were going to meet the six-month deadline, they were so imbued with energy and passion for achieving the goal that instead of saying, "Okay, now let's coast," they kept working on it every day to answer the questions "What is it that we've got in front of us to do, and is there a quicker way to accomplish it? How can we cut another day, another two days, another three days?"
>
> In the end, we even beat our six-month deadline, completing the source selection in less than five months. People were proud of themselves, and with good cause. When we talked about it afterwards, what the team discovered was that they hadn't known how capable they could be if they just quit thinking about things in the way they had always thought about them. They achieved what they did as a result of passion, commitment, and focus, as opposed to being smart. [47]

In their book *A Bias for Action*, Bruch and Ghoshal stress that willpower is crucial for forming an intention and for sustaining a commitment to achieve a specific challenging outcome. To protect commitment, the manager must take measures to control the environment, to keep out distractions, and to maintain focus [49]. In the two previous stories, Don and Terry invested much effort to sustain their teams' commitments by minimizing external interruptions.

In his book *Terms of Engagement*, Richard Axelrod discusses the pathways to commitment and explains that, initially, engagement may occur through the mind (e.g., being attracted to an idea) or the heart (e.g., an idea fitting one's value system), but the hands (e.g., the experience of working together to produce an outcome) actually sustain the commitment, and the commitment deepens as people begin to see the result of their work. Most importantly,

Axelrod wrote, the more that managers "walk their talk"—that is, their own behavior matches their expectations of their team—the more likely it is that their team will become highly committed [50].

Both Don and Terry "walked the talk" and were able to transform their projects and their teams. Did they demonstrate successful management or successful leadership? The outcomes were clearly extraordinary, the crews were clearly transformed, yet Terry's and Don's behavior did not include any specific act of leadership. They did not introduce any initiatives, attempt to challenge the status quo, or take risks. So, how did they transform their people? We believe that these two cases serve as great examples for the conclusion reached by Henry Mintzberg: "The best leadership is good management." Apparently, the genuine ownership and deep commitment exhibited continuously through the routine and engaging managerial behavior of Don and Terry served as a very effective influencing role model. By walking the talk, they were able to transform their teams [51].

❱❱ the role of the responsive agile project manager is to push the work and to pull the people

---

Leonard Sayles, who coined the term "working leaders" for managers like Don and Terry, concluded that "Leaders have two kinds of work: 'people' work and 'work' work." Adapting Sayles' definition, we may say that the role of the responsive agile project manager is to push the work and to pull the people. In the next chapter, we will discuss additional leadership roles played by successful project managers [52, 53].

Plumber: The Second Role of the Project Manager

James March, a renowned organization researcher from Stanford University concluded that "leadership involves plumbing as well as poetry." March explains that plumbing is "the capacity to apply known techniques effectively … keeping watch of the organization's efficiency in everyday tasks, such as making sure the toilets work and that there is somebody to answer the telephone. … This requires competence, not only at the top but also throughout all parts of the organization. … In order for the world to benefit from a few Don Quixotes and the rare Joans of Arc, it needs plenty of Sancho Panzas and Dunoises" [54, 55].

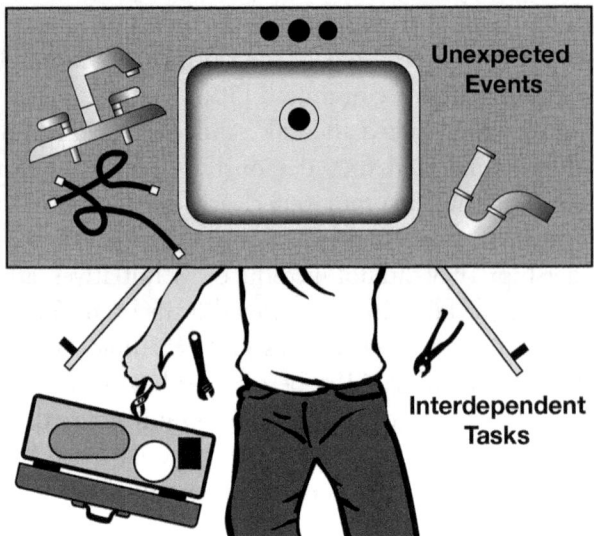

Fig. 3.4 The project manager must have the plumber's willingness to crawl below the leaking sink, if needs be, to solve problems as quickly as they emerge

March studied leadership in permanent organizations. But Leonard Sayles and Margaret Chandler, from Columbia University, who studied management and leadership in temporary organizations (i.e., projects), reached similar conclusions, that is, successful project managers are heavily engaged in everyday tasks. Moreover, they are highly responsive and action oriented. As noted earlier, due to the organizational structure of projects, in which tasks are tightly interconnected, when unexpected events affect one task, many other interdependent tasks may also be quickly impacted. Thus, solving problems as soon as they emerge is vital for maintaining work progress (Fig 3.4).

And so, the project manager must have the plumber's willingness to crawl below the leaking sink, if needs be, to solve problems as quickly as they emerge. The combination of technical competency and quick response allows successful project managers to be effective in their role as a plumber.

Key Points

- The project manager's key challenge today is coping with frequent unexpected events, and as such, project managers must have agility: quick *action during* the execution phase.
- Disseminating information frequently and routinely contributes to both flexibility and stability.

- Improvisation and fast, agile responses help keep projects running smoothly.
- Successful project managers strive to minimize the severity and duration of the impact of unexpected events in order to regain project stability as soon as possible and restart work according to the project plans.
- Moving about enables the project manager to disseminate information and to respond and act with agility.
- Managers who maintain a stationary position may be forced to make complex judgments with incomplete or misleading information.
- To ensure that moving about results in essential learning rather than destructive micromanagement, it must be accompanied by mutual trust.
- A successful project manager enables the team, allowing them to focus on their work and trusting their expertise and decisions.
- The second role of the successful project manager is as a plumber, willing to get his hands dirty by being highly responsive and action oriented.

References

1. Laufer, A. and Hoffman, E.J. *Project Management Success Stories: Lessons of Project Leaders.* 2000, New York: John Wiley & Sons: p. 76–8.
2. Aaltonen, K., Kujala, J., Lehtonen, P., and Ruuska, I. A Stakeholder Network Perspective on Unexpected Events and Their Management in International Projects. *International Journal of Managing Projects in Business* 2010; 3(4): p. 564–588.
3. Cavaleri, S., Firestone, J., and Reed, F. Managing Project Problem-Solving Patterns. *International Journal of Managing Projects in Business* 2012; 5(1): p. 125–145.
4. Coulon, T., Barki, H., and Paré, G. Conceptualizing Unexpected Events in IT projects, in *The 34th International Conference on Information Systems (ICIS).* 2013, Milano, Italy.
5. Geraldi, J.G., Lee-Kelley, L., and Kutsch, E. The Titanic Sunk, So What? Project Manager Response to Unexpected Events. *International Journal of Project Management* 2010; 28(6): p. 547–558.
6. Hällgren, M. and Lilliesköld, J. Three Modes of Deviation Handling: Coping with Unexpected Events in Project Management, in *Technology Management for the Global Future.* 2006, Istanbul, Turkey: PICMET.
7. Hällgren, M. and Maaninen-Olsson, E. Deviations and the Breakdown of Project Management Principles. *International Journal of Managing Projects in Business* 2009; 2(1): p. 53–69.
8. Holmberg, I. and Tyrstrup, M. Managerial Leadership as Event-Driven Improvisation, in *The Work of Managers: Towards a Practice Theory of Management,* S. Tengblad, Editor. 2012, Oxford: Oxford University Press: p. 47–68.

9. Piperca, S. and Floricel, S. A Typology of Unexpected Events in Complex Projects. *International Journal of Managing Projects in Business* 2012; 5(2): p. 248–265.

10. Söderholm, A. Project Management of Unexpected Events. *International Journal of Project Management* 2008; 26(1): p. 80–86.

11. Spetz, J., Keane, D., and Curry, S.A. Information Technology Implementation in a Rural Hospital: A Cautionary Tale. *Journal of Healthcare Management* 2009; 54(5): p. 337–341.

12. Tukiainen, S., Aaltonen, K., and Murtonen, M. Coping with an Unexpected Event: Project Managers' Contrasting Sensemaking in a Stakeholder Conflict in China. *International Journal of Managing Projects in Business* 2010; 3(3): p. 526–543.

13. Suchman, L.A. *Plans and Situated Actions: The Problem of Human-machine Communication.* 1987, Cambridge, UK: Cambridge University Press: p. vii.

14. Brooks Jr, F.P. *The Mythical Man-Month.* 1995, Reading, MA: Addison-Wesley: p. 240.

15. Mintzberg, H. Managerial Work: Analysis from Observation. *Management Science* 1971; 18(2): p. B-97–B-110.

16. Mintzberg, H. *The Nature of Managerial Work.* 1973, New York: Harper and Row: p. 71.

17. Laufer, A., Volkman, R.C., Davenport, G.W., and Terry, S. *In Quest of Project Excellence through Stories.* 1994, Cincinnati, OH: Procter and Gamble.

18. Boehm, B. and Turner, R. *Balancing Agility and Discipline: A Guide for the Perplexed.* 2003, Boston, MA: Addison-Wesley Professional: p. 34–5.

19. Majone, G. and Wildavsky, A.B. Implementation as Evolution, in *Implementation*, J.L. Pressman and A.B. Wildavsky, Editors. 1978, Berkeley, CA: University of California Press.

20. Schoenfelder, T.E. The Idyllic Workplace. *Ask Magazine* 2002; 7: p. 22–26.

21. Laufer, A., Hoffman, E.J., Russell, J.S., and Cameron, W.S. What Successful Project Managers Do. *MIT Sloan Management Review* 2015; 56(3): p. 43–51.

22. Laufer, A., Post, T., and Hoffman, E.J. *Shared Voyage: Learning and Unlearning from Remarkable Projects.* 2005, Washington, DC: The NASA History Series: p. 31.

23. Farjoun, M. Beyond Dualism: Stability and Change as a Duality. *Academy of Management Review* 2010; 35(2): p. 202–225.

24. Feldman, M.S. and Rafaeli, A. Organizational Routines as Sources of Connections and Understandings. *Journal of Management Studies* 2002; 39(3): p. 309–331.

25. Muirhead, B. and Simon, W.L. *High Velocity Leadership: The Mars Pathfinder Approach to Faster, Better, Cheaper.* 1999, New York: HarperBusiness: p. 193.

26. Weick, K.E. Organizational Redesign as Improvisation, in *Organizational Change and Redesign*, G.P. Huber and W.H. Glick, Editors. 1993, New York: Oxford University Press: p. 346–379.

27. Weick, K.E. Drop Your Tools: An Allegory for Organizational Studies. *Administrative Science Quarterly* 1996: p. 301–313.

28. Szalai, K. Fly Safe, but Fly. *Ask Magazine* 2004; 19: p. 12–15.

29. Laufer, A. and Hoffman, E.J. *Project Management Success Stories: Lessons of Project Leaders.* 2000, New York: John Wiley & Sons: p. 13–4.

30. Laufer, A. and Hoffman, E.J. *Project Management Success Stories: Lessons of Project Leaders.* 2000, New York: John Wiley & Sons: p. 82–5.

31. Leybourne, S. and Sadler-Smith, E. The Role of Intuition and Improvisation in Project Management. *International Journal of Project Management* 2006; 24(6): p. 483–492.

32. Miner, A.S., Bassof, P., and Moorman, C. Organizational Improvisation and Learning: A Field Study. *Administrative Science Quarterly* 2001; 46(2): p. 304–337.

33. Sayles, L.R. and Chandler, M.K. *Managing Large Systems: Organizations for the Future.* 1971, New York: Harper & Row: p. 218–9.

34. Amabile, T. and Kramer, S. *The Progress Principle.* 2011, Boston, MA: Harvard Business Review Press.

35. Boehm, B. and Turner, R. *Balancing Agility and Discipline: A Guide for the Perplexed.* 2004, Boston, MA: Addison-Wesley Professional: p. 25–57.

36. Meyer, B. *Agile: The Good, the Hype and the Ugly.* 2014, New York: Springer Science & Business Media.

37. Malhotra, Y. Knowledge Management for Organizational White Waters: An Ecological Framework. *Knowledge Management* 1999; 2(1): p. 18–21.

38. Roberto, M.A. *Know What You Don't Know: How Great Leaders Prevent Problems Before They Happen.* 2009, New Jersey: Pearson Prentice Hall: p. 193.

39. Peters, T.J. and Austin, N. *A Passion for Excellence. The Leadership Difference.* 1985, New York: Random House: p. 8–9.

40. Segal, E. *Doctors.* 1988, New York: Bantam Books: p. 303–6.

41. Bardnt, S.E. Upward Communication Filtering in the Project Management Environment. *Project Management Quarterly* 1981; 12(1): p. 39–43.

42. Mintzberg, H. *Rise and Fall of Strategic Planning.* 1994, New York: Free Press: p. 264–6.

43. Pfeffer, J. and Sutton, R.I. *The Knowing-Doing Gap: How Smart Companies Turn Knowledge into Action.* 1999, Boston, MA: Harvard Business Press: p. 139.

44. Laufer, A. and Hoffman, E.J. *Project Management Success Stories: Lessons of Project Leaders.* 2000, New York: John Wiley & Sons: p. 86–8.

45. Laufer, A., Post, T., and Hoffman, E.J. *Shared Voyage: Learning and Unlearning from Remarkable Projects.* 2005, Washington DC: The NASA History Series: p. 112–3.

46. Dorsey, Karen, Interview by Alex Laufer. 2010. (November).

47. Laufer, A. *Mastering the Leadership Role in Project Management Practices that Deliver Remarkable Results.* 2012, New Jersey: FT Press: p. 19–50.

48. Mintzberg, H. Managing. *BusinessWeek: Online Magazine.* 2009.

49. Bruch, H. and Ghoshal, S. *A Bias for Action: How Effective Managers Harness Their Willpower, Achieve Results, and Stop Wasting Time*. 2004, Boston, MA: Harvard Business Press.
50. Axelrod, R. *Terms of Engagement: New Ways of Leading and Changing Organizations*. 2010, Boston, MA: Berrett-Koehler Publishers.
51. Mintzberg, H. The Best Leadership Is Good Management. *Business Week: Online Magazine* 2009.
52. Katz, D. and Kahn, R.L. *The Social Psychology of Organizations*. 1978, New York: John Wiley & Sons: p. 528.
53. Sayles, L.R. A Different Perspective on Leadership: The Working Leader. *Leadership in Action* 1993; 13(1): p. 1–5.
54. Augier, M. James March on Education, Leadership, and Don Quixote: Introduction and Interview. *Academy of Management Learning & Education* 2004; 3(2): p. 169–177.
55. March, J.G. and Weil, T. *On Leadership*. 2009, New Jersey: John Wiley & Sons: p. 98.

4

The Resilience Practice: Challenge the Status Quo, Proactively Yet Selectively

"One man with courage makes a majority."
Andrew Jackson

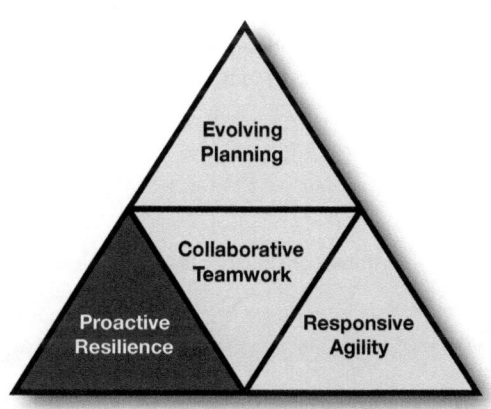

Challenge the Status Quo, Proactively

In today's dynamic environment, the problems that the project manager has to cope with during the life of a project can be classified into two categories: *technical* and *adaptive*. Most of the problems are technical—that is, they can be solved with knowledge and procedures already at hand. Coping with such

© The Author(s) 2018
A. Laufer et al., *Becoming a Project Leader*,
https://doi.org/10.1007/978-3-319-66724-9_4

problems was discussed in the previous chapter. Though solving technical problems may require great flexibility and high responsiveness, solving these problems can be done while maintaining the status quo. However, a few of the problems may not be well defined or have clear solutions, and often require fundamental changes in patterns of behavior. This chapter focuses on coping with such adaptive problems [1].

》in order to prevent a major disruption, the project manager must be willing to initiate a change rather than simply respond to events

---

To address adaptive problems, the project manager must demonstrate resilience by being willing to challenge the status quo, and very often do so proactively. That is, in order to prevent a major disruption, the project manager must be willing to initiate a change rather than simply respond to events. Because it is easier to tackle a threat before it reaches a full-blown state, a successful project manager acts as early as possible—as soon as he or she is convinced that a disruption is unavoidable (see Fig. 4.1) [2]. The following three examples feature project managers who proactively challenged the status quo.

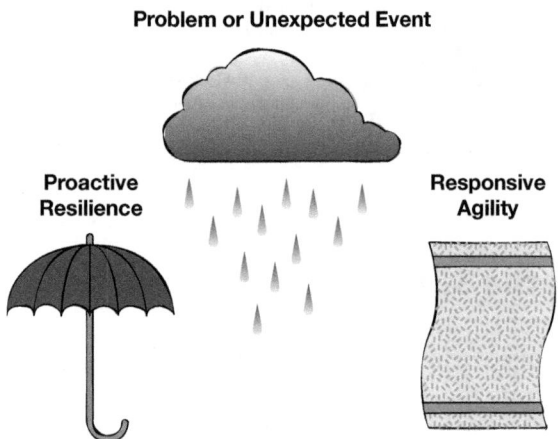

Problem or Unexpected Event

Proactive Resilience

Responsive Agility

Fig. 4.1 Responsive agility, discussed in the previous chapter, is about responding to unexpected events; proactive resilience is about prevention

Pre-crisis Intervention

In the first example, Don Margolies, who led NASA's Advanced Composition Explorer (ACE) project, attempted to influence the project's two most powerful stakeholders: the project's sponsor (NASA's upper leadership) and the project's clients (20 groups of scientists).

The project was plagued from the start with a string of financial issues arising from internal and external sources. Internally, the development of the nine scientific instruments led very quickly to a $22 million cost overrun. Externally, being part of the larger NASA Explorers program, the project inherited part of the budget overrun accrued in its preceding projects. As a result of these internal and external factors, the ACE project experienced frequent work stoppages, forcing Don to constantly change his contractors' and scientists' work priorities. Yet, these actions were not sufficient to resolve the financial problems.

Don concluded that unless he embarked on an uncommon and quite radical change, the project would continue down the same bumpy road, with the likely result that cost and time objectives would not be met. To prevent this, he made an extremely unpopular decision: He stopped the development of the instruments, calling on every science team to revisit its original technical requirements to see how they could be reduced. In every area—instruments, spacecraft, ground operation, integration and testing—scientists had to go back and ask basic questions, such as "How much can I save if I take out a circuit board?" and "How much performance will I lose if I do take it out?"

At the same time, Don negotiated a new agreement with NASA headquarters to secure stable funding, detached from the budget of the other six projects affiliated with the Explorers program. To seal the agreement, he assured them that by reducing his project's scope, it would not go over budget. With the reduced technical scope and the stable budget, the ACE project gradually overcame both its technical and organizational problems. Eventually, it was completed below budget, and the spacecraft has provided excellent scientific data ever since. [3]

Resilience has traditionally been seen as an ability to recover following a failure or a crisis. Recently, however, it has become accepted that by taking timely action before a disruption, organizations are able to change without first experiencing a crisis, and thus are able to introduce the change as cheaply as possible. By intervening prior to a major crisis, Don was being proactively resilient [4, 5].

New Stakeholders

At times, proactive resilience may call for adding new stakeholders to the project, then influencing them to act on behalf of the project. This was the creative solution employed by Jenny Baer-Riedhart, the leader of NASA's Environmental Research Aircraft and Sensor Technology (ERAST) project.

The goal of this rather atypical project for NASA was to test the conversion of Unmanned Aerial Vehicles (UAVs) into research platforms. In the middle of the project, Jenny's NASA team had to unexpectedly relocate from the Dryden Flight Research Center in California to the US Navy facility on the Hawaiian island of Kauai. Apparently, a key factor that led to the relocation was the reluctance of the human test pilots who dominated the Dryden Flight Center to provide precious airtime and flight resources for the unpiloted planes her project focused on. This, in fact, greatly hindered the progress of her project.

Although the flight test facilities at the Navy base on Kauai were fully capable of providing all the needed support, Jenny knew from bitter experience that this was not enough to ensure the success of the project. She felt that to be successful she would need to secure the support of not only the authorities at the Navy base but also of the residents of Kauai, who had a natural apprehension of outsiders. Thus, Jenny proactively directed her attention to winning over two stakeholders that did not even exist at the project's onset.

Jenny's search for an entrée into the Navy base and the surrounding community led to Dave, a former executive officer at the base. Dave was very willing to help, but he also had an unusual requirement: Jenny and all her team members, including NASA engineers and managers and the various contractors, would have to sing karaoke at his house. Jenny made sure that everyone attended. No one on her team had a Sinatra voice, but everyone managed to sing something; even painfully shy team members managed a few lines of "Happy Birthday." This won Dave over. He became the best marketing agent for the project.

Dave proceeded to smooth the way for Jenny's team by cutting through red tape in dealing with the Navy base authorities. He was also quick to let Hawaii's political machine know what was going on with their project, winning them over as well. At the same time, to help them establish a rapport with the local community, Dave introduced the team to Kauai's unique culture. They soon learned that Kauaians have high regard for those who educate their children. As part of the project's marketing strategy, the team developed educational programs in the schools and put together displays at the local museum. They also orchestrated an open house that was attended by approximately 1000 local schoolchildren, and students from Kauai Community College were hired to work on the project.

By the time the team left Kauai, they had probably spent 20 percent of their project time on these educational activities, but it all paid off: The local community was fully supportive of the project. Hawaii's entire congressional delegation sent a letter to NASA commending the team on the success of the program. Money that hadn't been previously available suddenly was approved. Less than six months after the move to Kauai, NASA's UAV broke the world record for solar-powered aircraft, flying to an altitude of 71,530 feet, with a flight time of more than 14 hours. [6]

Clearly, Dave was instrumental in bringing about the success of the project, but it was Jenny's foresight and recognition of the need for a stakeholder like Dave that enabled the team's success. Terry Little, a US Air Force project manager, also targeted a key stakeholder in his project management. But his approach was to influence the least powerful stakeholders: the contractors. To accomplish this, he had to challenge a long-held assumption of both the US Air Force's technical community and the contractors themselves.

After the first attempt was aborted due to a cost overrun of over $2 billion, the Pentagon had decided to make another stab at developing the Joint Air-to-Surface Standoff Missile (JASSM). Terry was then asked to replace the second attempt's original project manager, who was dismissed because of poor performance.

In an effort to keep costs under control, the Pentagon had decided to select two contractors and pay each one $200 million for the first two years of product development. The two contractors were to compete for the final $3 billion contract. But this unique contractual arrangement did not lead to a fundamental change in the contractors' product development approach. After several attempts to encourage the contractors to embrace an innovative change in the way they developed and manufactured the product, Terry came to the conclusion that unless he himself took a more radical approach, the contractors would not make the necessary shift in their project methodology, and the project would be canceled again. Therefore, he instructed the contractors to completely disregard most issued military standards and adopt only three key performance parameters.

One of the contractors, Lockheed Martin, took this directive seriously and changed its approach dramatically. It decided to build the missile fuselage not out of metal but out of composites. And to accomplish this, it found a company that made baseball bats and golf club shafts. The company had never built a military product, but it knew how to weave carbon fiber and was open minded. Following trials with several prototypes, this company was able to manufacture a product of the highest quality. Lockheed Martin transformed this small company from a baseball bat provider to a cruise missile supplier, which led to Lockheed Martin winning the contract (and also led to remarkable cost reductions). The eventual cost of a missile was $400,000, down from an expected $800,000. [7]

All three of these project managers exhibited proactive resilience, but the impact of their interventions differed. Don and Jenny were able to recover from their ongoing problems, preventing a major disruption, and each of them successfully met their project's objectives. As for Terry, he was not just able to meet his project's objectives; through his early intervention and radical approach, he was able to transform one of the teams and to cut the cost by half! [8]

Challenge the Status Quo, Selectively

As we've seen so far, it can be incredibly beneficial for managers to proactively challenge the status quo. Such proactive resilience requires anticipation and courage, elaborated upon in the next few sections. But we also wish to clarify that challenging the status quo is not the manager's primary job. Managing is. And so, after explaining the value of anticipation and courage, we subsequently advocate *selectively* challenging the status quo.

Anticipation: Embracing the Right Mindset

In their book *Great by Choice*, Jim Collins and Morten T. Hansen describe one of the core behaviors of great leaders as "productive paranoia." Even in calm periods, these leaders are considering the possibility that events could turn against them at any moment and are preparing to react. Similarly, successful project managers never stop expecting surprises, even though they may resort to major remedial changes only a few times during a project. They're constantly anticipating disruptions and maintaining the flexibility to respond proactively [9, 10].

》Anticipating does not mean predicting; rather, it means being on the lookout, attempting to be ready for the next difficult challenge

---

Anticipating does not mean predicting; rather, it means being on the lookout, attempting to be ready for the next difficult challenge. Here is how Allan Frandsen at the California Institute of Technology describes the importance of the ongoing process of anticipation:

> In running a project, I have always tried to anticipate problems. … If I had to write down the ABCs of project management, "A" would signify anticipation. … Of course, a good project manager already knows, at least in general terms,

what is supposed to happen next—but all too often it doesn't. So what are the alternatives? Are there sensible work-arounds? What can I do now to lay the groundwork or facilitate matters should something go wrong? These and other questions make up the ongoing process of anticipation. And because it is an ongoing process, the "A" in the ABCs of project management could just as well stand for "anticipate … anticipate … anticipate." [11]

In his book *Streetlights and Shadows*, Gary Klein explains, "Anticipatory thinking lets us manage our attention so that we are looking in the right places to spot anomalies in case they appear." It is important to note that in the process of anticipation, successful project managers rely less on large "databases" associated with the project planning and control systems and more on "small data" that results from their "moving-about activities," briefly meeting face-to-face with a variety of people and observing firsthand many small incidents and anomalies (described in Chap. 3) [12–15].

Don Margolies, the ACE project manager discussed earlier in this chapter, relied primarily on the "small data" approach while attempting to anticipate problems that might require an early major intervention. Since his annual budget was dependent on resources available from the Explorers Program, Don took the time to meet with several project managers affiliated with that program as well as with a few officials from NASA headquarters. Don also met with vendors who were supplying services to his project as well as to other projects in the Explorers Program. Through these brief and often informal meetings, Don concluded that the cost overruns of several projects affiliated with the Explorers Program were likely to increase in the near future, while the overall budget of the Explorers Program would probably not grow. Combining this information with the overruns expected by most of the science groups in his own project, he realized that he needed to take immediate action to prevent a major project disruption.

»It can't be stressed enough that noticing problems before they occur requires a special mindset

---

It can't be stressed enough that noticing problems before they occur requires a special mindset. Here is how Jim Collins describes this mindset in his book *Great by Choice*: "The 10X companies (companies beating their industry indexes by a minimum of 10 times over 15 years) differ from their less successful companies in how they maintain hypervigilance in good times as well as in bad. Even in calm, clear, positive conditions, 10Xers constantly consider

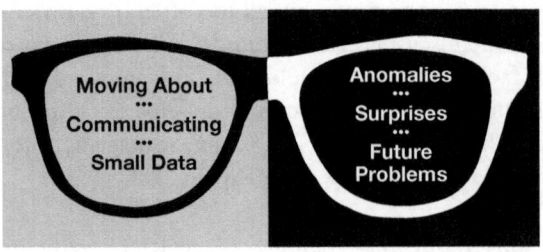

Fig. 4.2 Successful project managers have one "paranoid" eye on anomalies, surprises, and future problems; and the other eye on the small data that might enable them to anticipate disruptions

the possibility that events could turn against them at any moment. ... And they'd better be prepared."

Collins calls this mindset "productive paranoia" because the continuous fear of future disruptions is channeled into readiness to take productive action [9].

Likewise, the successful project managers we studied constantly searched for signs of anomalies, of surprises, of future major problems, while leading a project review session, while visiting workstations during their frequent moving-about tours, as well as while communicating often with their clients. However, readiness to take action requires more than a mindset of "productive paranoia," it requires also "the capacity to act." Karl Weick, a renowned organization researcher, stresses that the ability to notice disruptions early on is not detached from the ability to cope with these disruptions. As he puts it, "When you develop the capacity to act on something, then you can afford to see it" [16–18] (Fig. 4.2).

Courage: Choosing Your Battles

Studying dozens of successful project managers during the last two decades, we have come to realize that challenging the status quo creatively and courageously frequently changes the fate of a project and is widely regarded as a key component of project leadership [19–21]. In their book *Fusion Leadership*, Daft and Lengel have this to say: "Leadership in a destabilized world means nonconformity. One obvious trait that distinguishes a leader from a manager is a willingness to take risks. ... It takes courage to jump into a new way of doing things" [22].

In the three examples described earlier in this chapter, the project managers exhibited courage by their willingness, and ability, to convince their teams to do things in a new way. Don Margolies exhibited courage when he went against his 20 science teams, forcing them to significantly reduce the technical scope of the project so that he could secure a stable budget. Jenny Baer-Riedhart convinced her entire team to sing karaoke in order to obtain the marketing services of Dave, whereas Terry Little guided his contractors to disregard the military standards so that they would feel free to innovate.

Although courage is regarded by many authorities as a key component of leadership, like many good things, too much courage may at times have a corrosive impact, as illustrated in the following story by Terry Little.

> I've made plenty of mistakes in my career, but the one that I think of as providing the greatest learning opportunities occurred while I was program manager of a large Department of Defense (DoD) project designated by Congress as an acquisition reform program. I was told I would have my department's support to try almost anything—so long as it wasn't illegal—to improve acquisition in the DoD.
>
> One of the things that came to me was to emulate a practice used by many commercial companies: profit sharing. I wanted to establish a way for the people working for me to share in the savings of the program. As I saw it, it was a win-win situation.
>
> I was sure the savings were going to be enormous, and I believed it would stimulate my people to be more creative, innovative, and give them a greater sense of ownership over the outcome of the program. Thus, I set off on my Don Quixote quest to get approval.
>
> When I went back to tell the people in my department my ideas about pay-for-performance incentives, I found their reaction to be a little too cool for my taste. But I already had fallen in love with my idea and was determined to get approval at the Pentagon no matter what. I commenced to making trips from Florida to Washington DC every week, talking to various people in the Pentagon, explaining what I had in mind and why it was such a wonderful idea. … Over the next two years, I spent almost half my time in Washington.
>
> So carried away did I get with my brilliant idea that I decided to try and see the Secretary of Defense himself. I managed to get an appointment on his calendar for a 15-minute meeting. I explained my proposal. He listened and then he said, "Well, I need to talk with my staff about this." When he said this to me, I knew that I was finished because the people he was going to talk with were the same people I had talked with before I got to see him.
>
> After this was all over, I looked back and realized that it was my own fault that the program experienced so many difficulties. I focused on my one pet idea and neglected much else. I felt disgusted with myself. I thought constantly about what I had done, how I could be so stupid. For a year, it made me draw in and not want to push anymore, it made me timid and risk-averse, and that is a crippling state of mind to be in for a project manager. [23]

In this remarkable story, Terry candidly shares the mistakes he made in an attempt to proactively impact the success of his project. Concluding his story,

Terry describes three major lessons he learned and would implement in future projects. First, it is important to carefully choose one's battles. Second, while it is legitimate to take a wrong turn, it is important to know when to retreat. One should employ self-discipline to ensure timely retreat. Failing this step may be detrimental to the progress of the project. Finally, being resilient entails the ability to recover quickly after a failure, and to achieve this, one must learn to forgive oneself. As Terry explained several years later, following a setback in a different project,

> It would be nice if failures never happened, but any time you undertake something that has significant risk, no matter how well you attempt to do it, no matter what the caliber of the team, no matter how much money you have to spend, there will always be times when you have failures.... Whenever there is a failure, the first thing to do is to go through a short grieving period. On JASSM, whenever we had a failure, I allowed grieving for one day. We could grieve and mope, get drunk, wring our hands, say "ain't it awful." We could do that for one day, and then it was time to put it behind us. That's a Terry Little rule. [11]

Terry Little's Lessons on Resilience

► Choose your battles

► Employ self-discipline in retreating from missteps

► Forgive yourself after a failure

Just Enough Leadership

Is there a common leadership philosophy, shared by the successful project managers we studied, that can help us better understand how and when courageous behavior is beneficial in today's dynamic environment?

In a famous essay, Oxford philosopher Isaiah Berlin described two approaches to life, using a simple parable about a fox and a hedgehog. The fox is cunning and creative, able to devise a myriad of complex strategies to attack the hedgehog. The hedgehog is painfully slow, with a very simple daily agenda: searching for food and maintaining his home. Every day, the fox waits for the hedgehog while planning to attack him. When the hedgehog senses the danger, he reacts in the same simple, but powerful, way: He rolls up into a perfect little ball, with a sphere of sharp spikes pointing outward in all directions. Then the fox retreats while starting to plan his new line of attack for the next day. Each day, this confrontation takes place, and despite the greater cunning of the fox, the hedgehog always wins [24].

Based on this parable, Berlin attempted to divide the world into two basic groups: foxes and hedgehogs. Foxes pursue many ends at the same time, yet they do not integrate their thinking into one overall concept. Hedgehogs, on the other hand, simplify a complex world into a single overall concept that unifies and guides everything they do.

In recent years, several prominent management scholars have discussed this parable while attempting to answer the following question: Do successful senior managers behave more like hedgehogs or like foxes? The debate regarding senior managers is still going on, but when it comes to successful project managers, we have found that they perform both like hedgehogs and foxes, although they embrace the hedgehog's behavior more prominently [25–28].

» Managers in successful projects feel a total personal accountability for results

Like the hedgehog, managers in successful projects were guided by one overriding purpose: delivering successful results to the customer. They clearly felt a sense of ownership of the project, both an intellectual and emotional bond. For them, the project objectives were not simply the technical definition of the customer's needs. Objectives meant, first of all, results, and they felt a total personal accountability for those results. This commitment also meant that they had the self-discipline to make all other objectives and opportunities secondary. It was almost as if they were programmed to follow an inner compass that was always pointing toward true north. However, if they could not reach this goal by following conventional methods, they responded by challenging the status quo. This kind of response requires strong willpower and courage.

It is important to note that this focus on delivering results to the customer was also why these project managers challenged the status quo only occasionally. They knew very well that challenging the status quo has its own risks and costs. In particular, it would require that they dedicate special attention and energy to overcoming the natural resistance to their intervention. The resulting disequilibrium in the project could lead to a loss of momentum and progress, eventually hurting their ability to serve the customer. Because their primary focus was not on proving that they were heroes but on delivering results to the customer, their hedgehog's mentality guided them in selecting only the vital cases in which to challenge the status quo.

And now to the role of the fox. It is evident from the projects we studied that while it was the project managers' focused willpower that led them to

Fig. 4.3 By embracing the behavior of both the hedgehog and the fox, the project manager can successfully challenge the status quo when the need arises

challenge the status quo, the solutions to the problems they faced demanded a great deal of adaptability and creativity. That is when the focused hedgehog calls on the creative fox for help. It's the fox that is able to disregard military standards or bring in a karaoke-enthusiast stakeholder. By embracing the behavior of both the hedgehog and the fox, the project manager can successfully challenge the status quo when the need arises (Fig. 4.3).

In summary, to focus on delivering results to the customer, successful project managers make sure that although they may have to challenge the status quo on occasion, they will do so selectively. As Henry Mintzberg concludes in a recent Harvard Business Review article, "So maybe it's time to wean ourselves from the heroic leader and recognize that actually we need *just enough leadership*" [29].

Entrepreneur: The Third Role of the Project Manager

The entrepreneurship literature highlights several key characteristics common to successful entrepreneurs: They constantly seek opportunities; they are innovative and proactive as they engage in developing and selling their ideas;

and they are resilient and ready to cope with failures while they are challenging the status quo.

The examples throughout our chapter demonstrate that successful project managers act like entrepreneurs, though rather than seek opportunities, they constantly look out for potential threats. In attempting to cope with disruptions before they've occurred, they are very similar to entrepreneurs. Like entrepreneurs, they are innovative and proactive, engaged in developing and selling their ideas for coping with future threats; they are also resilient and ready to cope with failures (Fig. 4.4).

This third role, entrepreneur, is performed alongside the project manager's other two roles, which were discussed in Chaps. 2 and 3: decision choreographer and plumber. In the next section, we will highlight how these three roles complement each other [30–33].

Fig. 4.4 Like entrepreneurs, successful project managers are innovative and proactive, engaged in developing and selling their ideas for coping with future threats; they are also resilient and ready to cope with failures

Lead, So You Can Manage

Throughout the first four chapters of this book, we have provided multiple illustrations showing that today's project managers have to constantly cope with one or more of the following challenges:

- Changes resulting from the dynamic *environment* surrounding today's projects.
- Difficulties of coping with challenging *requirements* and radical *constraints*, as well as with sudden changes in these requirements and constraints.
- Surprises resulting from the unique and often innovative project *tasks*.
- Numerous *unexpected events* and *problems* subsequent to the above difficulties.
- Difficulties in coping with these problems due to the typically unique, temporary, and evolving *project organization*, which is composed of heterogeneous units.

It is therefore not surprising that in performing their roles as decision choreographer, plumber, and entrepreneur, project managers focus on coping with changes. As Table 4.1 indicates, the decision choreographer deals with deviations from the plans, the agile plumber focuses on unexpected events, and the resilient entrepreneur attempts to prevent major threats. Looking at the two first roles of the project manager, one cannot resist asking the question: How can project managers assume two such contradictory approaches—*stability* (planning) and *flexibility* (agility)?

Table 4.1 Coping with different changes through planning, agility, and resilience

Mode of coping with change / Change Characteristics	Evolving planning (Decision Choreographer)	Responsive agility (Plumber)	Proactive resilience (Entrepreneur)
Nature of changes	Deviations from plans	Unexpected events	Major threats
Timing of identifying changes	Periodically	Continuously	Occasionally
Timing of coping with changes	Periodically	As soon as the problem is identified	Proactively, once a future threat becomes imminent
Primary purpose for coping with changes	To execute the project according to the updated project plan	To maintain forward momentum	To prevent major disruptions

In recent years, the "stability-flexibility paradox" has been dealt with extensively by researchers, consultants, and practitioners. In his book *The Age of Paradox*, the British executive and researcher Charles Handy discusses the paradox of organizations and concludes the following: "The successful [organizations] live with paradox. … Firms have to be planned yet flexible. … They have to reconcile what used to be opposites, instead of choosing between them." Similarly, in his book *Rules of Thumb*, Alan Webber, the former editorial director of the *Harvard Business Review*, concludes, "These are extraordinary times. … It's time to re-write the rules. … We've moved from an either/or past to a both/and future" [34, 35].

As discussed in Chap. 3, successful project managers employ the agile approach to cope with routine problems as soon as they are identified. Their primary purpose is to continue project implementation by following the plans and thus maintain forward momentum. That is, they employ the *agile (flexibility)* approach so they can quickly rely again on the planning approach (*stability*).

At the same time, without planning (*stability*), it is impossible to practice agility (*flexibility*) effectively. As claimed by Karl Weick, "flexibility without stability results in chaos" [36]. Likewise, a group of consultants, the Price Waterhouse Change Integration Team, claimed that positive change requires significant stability. In their book *The Paradox Principles*, they wrote the following: "Most of the managers we've interviewed believe this to be true: People detest uncertainty. … At a time when we are bombarded by the message of change, when management gurus get rich with books advocating chaos … it seems almost cowardly to talk of stability. … We disagree with this attitude emphatically. Resolutely" [37].

Similarly, the successful project managers we have studied continuously employed flexible practices but were acutely aware that their teams could not cope with too much change and flexibility. They performed much better by resorting again and again, very quickly, to project planning and stability. In fact, these project managers felt that planning and agility do not just coexist, they are complementary and mutually enabling.

» Successful project managers *lead* (occasionally) in order to *manage* (most of the time)

And now to another apparent tension embedded in Table 4.1: management versus leadership. In their first two roles, decision choreographer and plumber, project managers deal primarily with routine issues and do not have to challenge the status quo. Thus, for most of the time (periodically for the decision choreographer, continuously for the plumber), successful project managers assume a managerial role. In contrast, in their third role, entrepreneur, they occasionally have to deal with non-routine problems and at times must challenge the status quo, assuming a leadership role. Following our previous analysis of the hedgehog and the fox, and adopting Henry Mintzberg's "Just Enough Leadership" guideline, we may easily resolve this apparent tension. Successful project managers *lead* (occasionally) in order to *manage* (most of the time). In the next chapter, we explain how blending the three roles of the project manager (decision choreographer, plumber, and entrepreneur) is facilitated and maintained by teamwork.

Key Points

- Proactive resilience is about initiating change rather than simply responding to events, and it often requires challenging the status quo.
- Intervening prior to a major crisis and creatively enlisting new stakeholders can help prevent problems.
- Great leaders have "productive paranoia": they're always considering how things could go wrong.
- Courage means not only taking risks in challenging the status quo, but also recovering from failures and wrong turns.
- Successful project managers have a hedgehog's focus on results and fox's resourcefulness when challenging the status quo is necessary.
- In attempting to cope with disruptions before they've occurred, project managers are very similar to entrepreneurs.
- Stability and flexibility must not only coexist, but also be complementary and mutually enabling.
- Successful project managers lead (occasionally) in order to manage (most of the time).

References

1. Heifetz, R.A. and Linsky, M. *Leadership on the Line*. 2002, Boston: Harvard Business School Press.
2. Sheremata, W.A. Finding and Solving Problems in Software New Product Development. *Journal of Product Innovation Management* 2002; 19(2): p. 144–158.

3. Laufer, A. *Mastering the Leadership Role in Project Management: Practices that Deliver Remarkable Results*. 2012, New Jersey: FT Press: p. 171–192.

4. Comfort, L.K., Boin, A., and Demchak, C.C. *Designing Resilience: Preparing for Extreme Events*. 2010, Pittsburgh, PA: University of Pittsburgh Press.

5. Välikangas, L. *The Resilient Organization: How Adaptive Cultures Thrive Even When Strategy Fails*. 2010, USA: McGraw Hill Professional.

6. Laufer, A. *Mastering the Leadership Role in Project Management: Practices that Deliver Remarkable Results*. 2012, New Jersey: FT Press: p. 71–102.

7. Laufer, A. *Mastering the Leadership Role in Project Management: Practices that Deliver Remarkable Results*. 2012, New Jersey: FT Press: p. 19–50.

8. Westrum, R. A Typology of Resilience Situations, in *Resilience Engineering: Concepts and Precepts*, E. Hollnagel, D.D. Woods, and N. Leveson, Editors. 2006, Boca Raton, FL: CRC Press: p. 55–65.

9. Collins, J. and Hansen, M.T. *Great by Choice: Uncertainty, Chaos and Luck-Why Some Thrive Despite Them All*. 2011, New York: Random House.

10. Grove, A.S. *Only the Paranoid Survive: How to Exploit the Crisis Points that Challenge Every Company*. 1996, New York: Currency Doubleday.

11. Laufer, A., Post, T., and Hoffman, E.J. *Shared Voyage: Learning and Unlearning from Remarkable Projects*. 2005, Washington, DC: The NASA History Series.

12. Klein, G. *Streetlights and Shadows*. 2009, Cambridge: MIT Press.

13. Klein, G., Snowden, D., and Pin, C.L. Anticipatory thinking, in *Informed by Knowledge: Expert Performance in Complex Situations*, K.L. Mosier and U.M. Fischer, Editors. 2011, New York: Psychology Press: p. 235–246.

14. Lindstrom, M. *Small Data: The Tiny Clues that Uncover Huge Trends*. 2016, New York: St. Martin's Press.

15. McLennan, J., Elliot, G., and Holgate, A. Anticipatory Thinking and Managing Complex Tasks: Wildfire Fighting Safety and Effectiveness, in *Proceedings of the Industrial & Organisational Psychology Conference*. 2009, Sydney: Australian Psychological Society.

16. Bazerman, M. *The Power of Noticing: What the Best Leaders See*. 2014, New York: Simon and Schuster.

17. Rate, C.R. and Sternberg, R.J. When Good People Do Nothing: A Failure of Courage, in *Research Companion to the Dysfunctional Workplace: Management Challenges and Symptoms*, J. Langan-Fox, C.L. Cooper, and R.J. Klimoski, Editors. 2007, Cheltenham, UK: Edward Elgar Publishing: p. 3–21.

18. Weick, K.E. Drop Your Tools: On Reconfiguring Management Education. *Journal of Management Education* 2007; 31(1): p. 5–16.

19. Laufer, A. *Breaking the Code of Project Management*. 2009, New York: Palgrave Macmillan.

20. Laufer, A. *Mastering the Leadership Role in Project Management: Practices that Deliver Remarkable Results*. 2012, New Jersey: FT Press.

21. Laufer, A. and Hoffman, E.J. *Project Management Success Stories: Lessons of Project Leaders*. 2000, New York: Wiley.

22. Daft, R.L. and Lengel, R.H. *Fusion Leadership: Unlocking the Subtle Forces that Change People and Organizations.* 1998, San Francisco, CA: Berrett-Koehler Publishers.

23. Little, T. The Don Quixote Complex. *Ask Magazine* 2001; 5: p. 12–14.

24. Berlin, I. *The Hedgehog and the Fox: An Essay on Tolstoy's View of History.* 1953, UK: Weidenfeld and Nicolson.

25. Collins, J. *Good to Great: Why Some Companies Make the Leap... and Others Don't.* 2001, New York: HarperCollins.

26. Gardner, D. *Future Babble: Why Expert Predictions Fail-and Why We Believe Them Anyway.* 2010, Toronto, Ontario: McClelland & Stewart.

27. Grint, K. The Hedgehog and the Fox: Leadership Lessons from D-Day. *Leadership* 2014; 10(2): p. 240–260.

28. Zaleznik, A. *Hedgehogs and Foxes.* 2008, New York: Palgrave Macmillan.

29. Mintzberg, H. Rebuilding Companies as Communities. *Harvard Business Review* 2009; 87(7/8): p. 140–143.

30. Berkun, S. *The Myths of Innovation.* 2010, Sebastopol, CA: O'Reilly Media.

31. Bessant, J. and Tidd, J. *Innovation and Entrepreneurship.* 2007, UK: John Wiley & Sons.

32. Murphy, B. *The Intelligent Entrepreneur: How Three Harvard Business School Graduates Learned the 10 Rules of Successful Entrepreneurship.* 2010, New York: Henry Holt & Co.

33. Sarasvathy, S.D. *Effectuation: Elements of Entrepreneurial Expertise.* 2008, Cheltenham, UK: Edward Elgar Publishing.

34. Handy, C. *The Age of Paradox.* 1995, US: Harvard Business Press.

35. Webber, A.M. *Rules of Thumb: 52 Truths for Winning at Business Without Losing Your Self.* 2009, New York: HarperCollins.

36. Weick, K.E. Management of Organizational Change Among Loosely Coupled Elements, in *Change in Organizations: New perspectives on Theory, Research, and Practice,* P.S. Goodman, Editor. 1982, New York: Jossey-Bass: p. 375–408.

37. Price Waterhouse Change Integration Team. *The Paradox Principles: How High Performance Companies Manage Chaos, Complexity and Contradictions to Achieve Superior Results.* 1996, Chicago: Irwin Professional Publisher.

5

Collaborative Teamwork: Cultivate and Sustain Collaboration by Focusing on the Individual, the Team, and the Work

"There are no problems we cannot solve together, and very few that we can solve by ourselves."
Lyndon B. Johnson

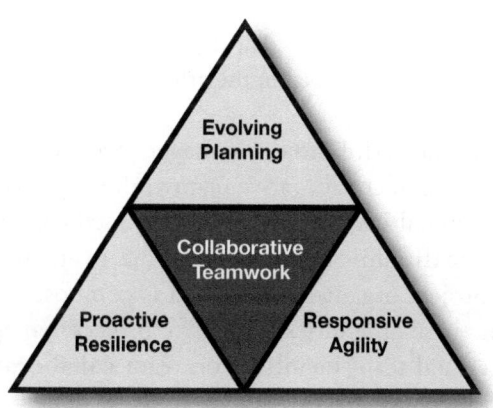

In 1911, Fredrick Taylor, the father of "scientific management," said, "In the past man has been first. In the future the system must be first" [1]. Taylor's approach has dominated managerial thinking throughout most of the twentieth century. More recently, a fundamental shift has taken place, as eloquently stated in 1999 by Kevin Kelly, the founding executive editor of *Wired* maga-

© The Author(s) 2018
A. Laufer et al., *Becoming a Project Leader*,
https://doi.org/10.1007/978-3-319-66724-9_5

zine: "the [current] network economy is founded on technology, but can only be built on relationships. It starts with chips and ends with trust" [2].

Since project progress depends on the contribution of individuals who represent different disciplines and are affiliated with different parties, collaboration is particularly important in project management. It is imperative for the early detection of problems as well as for the quick development and smooth implementation of appropriate solutions. The crucial role of collaboration can be demonstrated by the following example of projects which were considered failures.

> Tim Flores analyzed the causes for the different outcomes of three Mars exploration missions initiated by NASA's Jet Propulsion Laboratory: Pathfinder, Climate Orbiter, and Polar Lander. Although all three projects were conducted under the same guiding principles, were of comparable scope and shared many elements (even some of the same team members), Pathfinder was a success, whereas the other two missions failed. Flores expected to find that the Pathfinder project differed from the other projects in a variety of factors, such as resources, constraints, and personnel. Although this was true to some extent, he found that the primary factor distinguishing the successful mission from the failed missions was the level of collaboration. The Pathfinder team developed trusting relationships within a culture of openness. Managers felt free to make the best decisions they could, and they knew that they weren't going to be crucified for mistakes. That trust never developed in the other two projects. [3]

Through studying successful project managers, we found that they are well aware of the crucial role of collaborative teamwork for project success, as well as of the difficulties in cultivating and sustaining such teamwork. These difficulties result from the dynamic nature of the project's environment, and from the ever-evolving project organization, which is composed of heterogeneous units. To overcome these difficulties, successful project managers focus on the suitability of **individual** team members, on team **collaboration**, and on the **work** and its outcomes (Fig. 5.1).

Focus on the Suitability of the Individual Team Members

In his book, *Good to Great: Why Some Companies Make the Leap ... and Others Don't*, which has sold over 2.5 million hardcover copies and has been translated into 32 languages, Jim Collins reports that one of the principles practiced by most successful companies was "First who ... then what." As Collins explains, "We expect that good-to-great leaders would begin by setting a new

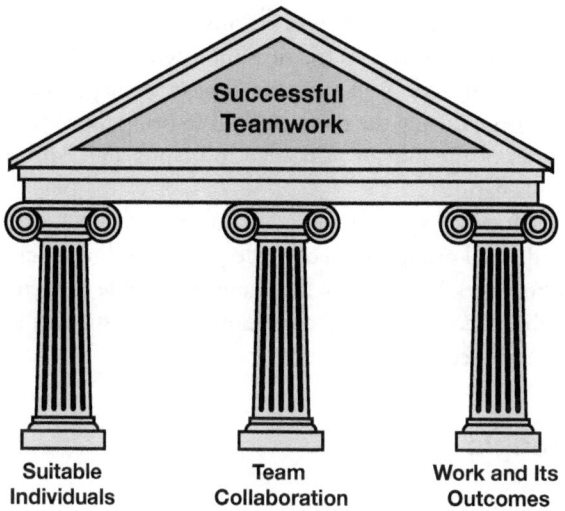

Fig. 5.1 The three pillars of collaboration: the suitability of the individuals, the collaboration of the team, and the focus on the work and its outcomes

vision and strategy. We found instead that they **first** got the right people on the bus, the wrong people off the bus, and the right people in the right seats—and **then** they figured out where to drive it" [4].

James Kilts (former Chairman and CEO of the Gillette Company) and his colleagues reach a similar conclusion in their book *Doing What Matters*: "People are the make-or-break factor in business. With the right people, almost anything is possible. With the wrong team, failure awaits" [5].

Recruiting Team Members

In the following example, Ken Schwer, a Project Manager from NASA, describes the great efforts that were required for recruiting his team. His story highlights how recruiting has changed from being like purchasing (of resources) by Human Resources to selling (the project) by the project manager:

A project manager is only as good as his/her staff, so it was important for me to concentrate on selecting my core team. Since the clock to Solar Dynamics Observatory (SDO) launch had started, I needed key individuals on board to make progress. I believe "Hand picking" the core team is an important part of establishing a teamwork environment. I wouldn't leave staffing key positions to chance.

I knew that it was important to work with the functional supervisors and not bypass them when it came to staffing. I needed their approval and cooperation if SDO was to be successful. But I also knew that people being recruited often need to know the answers to many questions before they are ready to make a commitment to a new project. Is the mission interesting? How will the project operate and be organized? Will you, the project manager, be someone I can receive support from during the time required to bring the SDO dreams to reality? As the leader of the mission, I needed to be prepared with the answers for questions of this nature ....

To accomplish this, I spent many many hours each week sitting down with individuals and small groups to go over the project and to solicit their support. As a result, I became a better salesperson, and I was able to identify and recruit the most suitable candidates as my core team with the support and approval of functional management. [6]

The Right People

While there is an almost-unanimous agreement regarding the need to recruit the "right" people, there is no agreement regarding the criteria that define those "right" people. When it comes to projects, however, one thing is very clear: "right" does not mean "stars." Indeed, one of the primary reasons for project "dream teams" to fail is "signing too many all-stars." As Geoffrey Colvin, *Fortune*'s senior editor-at-large, explains, "If everybody is a potential CEO, it's difficult to have an effective team" [7].

In his essay "Teams and Stars," Scott Berkun elaborates on the "myth of all-star teams":

"The true goal of any team is not to have the best players for each position: it's to succeed. Success comes when a team makes use of the team's abilities towards a goal, something you don't get merely by picking the best players at each position. It's a rookie mistake: you can't hire assuming people will work alone. You have to understand how each person will interact and collaborate with others and choose people that fit (or that create useful tensions that you carefully manage)" [8].

The following case is a vivid example of how an individual who is not necessarily an all-star expert is the "dream team member" of any project manager. Frank Snow, the Ground System and Flight Operations Manager at NASA's Goddard Space Flight Center, recalls one of his most remarkable team members:

Officially, Chuck Athas was listed as my scheduler and planner. In the beginning of a project, we put together an extensive schedule. Maintaining the schedule, however, did not take up all of his time, and he was constantly looking for work.

Chuck would do anything I asked—and then some things I didn't dare to ask. All I had to do was put it out there that we had a problem. For example, when people weren't meeting a particular deadline, I could send out emails and phone messages, and they would conveniently not be around to respond. I could say to Chuck, "Go and find out what's happening," and he would be on it right away. If someone was slacking off or had issues they didn't want to fess up to, Chuck could turn things around just by virtue of his personality. I saw him work this way and it was magical. He never resorted to being confrontational, but boy could he lay a guilt trip on you: "You have to get it done. What do you mean? You're committed to this. The whole program is going to collapse."

It was impossible to argue with Chuck. He would say, "Let me help you. I'll do anything." When someone would say, "I don't have the time," Chuck would come back with, "I'll do it, what do you need done?" "Well, I have to get my daughter out of daycare." Chuck's answer was, "I'll get your daughter out of daycare." Whatever needed to be done, he'd do it for you—anything.

I used Chuck to keep in contact with a guy named Chris, one of the engineers at the Johns Hopkins Applied Physics Laboratory (APL). Chris was very popular at Goddard. He was one-of-a-kind, an absolute genius, and usually spread out over 15 to 20 projects. If Chris couldn't solve a problem, then we were in trouble. I would send Chris e-mails, leave him phone messages, and try contacting his supervisors—nothing. I can't say that he was definitely trying to avoid me, but he was probably trying to avoid me. But I also knew that if you could physically get hold of Chris, he would do your work. So it was Chuck's job to go over there, get ahold of Chris and bring him back to me. I used to say to Chuck, "Find Chris because I absolutely need him," and Chuck would go to APL and literally sit outside of Chris's door until he showed up.

Chuck was also like the master sergeant in the army who has the inside knowledge of how to get supplies. Somehow things showed up and nobody understood how they appeared. They certainly weren't coming through procurement. He was trading, I suspect. I know that he used up a lot of the little things that we get for projects, like decals and posters. One time we needed six or seven headsets for communications on mission simulations. As the simulations approached, they still hadn't been delivered. I called Chuck and told him the problem, and he got it resolved. To tell you the truth, I don't know how he got them. And to be honest, I don't want to know.

Anything that needed to be done, and he didn't care what it was, he would attack with the same gusto and unflappable drive to succeed. Whatever it took to get the job done, Chuck would do. Don't ask, don't tell. That was the best way I found to deal with Chuck. Was there anything he couldn't make happen? Probably something. But with Chuck on the team I felt like I could ask for Cleveland, and the next day he would show up with the deed. [9]

» His adherence to the project goals over his own goals made him an ideal team member

Chuck demonstrated a lack of ego that most all-stars don't have. His adherence to the project goals over his own goals made him an ideal team member. Terry Little, a project manager from the US Air Force, asserts that "If you pick the right guy, everything can be screwed up and you will still be successful. I therefore spend a lot of time picking the right horse to ride on." In the following story, Terry Little highlights the importance and the difficulties in adhering to Jim Collins's rule that "People are **not** your most important asset, the **right** people are."

When requested to lead a $1 billion highly classified project for the Pentagon, I was told I could select whomever I wanted to work with me and that I would have the freedom to ignore all rules and regulations; the only stipulations were that I had to obey the law and keep the team very small. Little did I know what learning, heartbreak, and exhilaration this would bring. I cannot write about the thrills and heartbreak because of security, but I would like to share what I learned and unlearned.

My first task was to pick the people who would be on the team. I had had people work for me before in the military, but I never had the luxury of picking them. I immediately began interviewing candidates whom I thought might be suitable. I was able to eliminate some interviewees right away. They were the ones most interested in whether or not they would get promoted and those who were eager to tell me how bad their current boss was. I also eliminated anyone whose primary concern was how hard they would have to work.

After my initial screen, my major criteria were to pick people who were very experienced, understood the complicated acquisition processes in the Department of Defense and who were skillful in their respective functions. That turned out to be a critical mistake. Many of those I picked using those criteria were very poor performers. Most left voluntarily (this was easy because I had a policy that anyone on the team could leave anytime for any reason. True, I made sure poor performers knew they were not doing well and why).

Why they were poor performers is informative. One of the most salient reasons was that some cared more about following the processes and avoiding risks than they did about achieving the project's objectives. I am not sure why this was. My hypothesis is that some people need clear rules and are hypersensitive to the potential of making mistakes. It was as if the limit of their accountability was process accountability and not project outcome accountability. I concluded that some people are simply unable to adapt to an ambiguous, rapidly changing project environment.

Another key, related reason was that some poor performers were simply not team players. A couple spent enormous energy criticizing the contractor and bloviating, but did very little work. A few very experienced team members seemed to have been unable to apply that experience to a different situation. They appeared to be handicapped by their experience rather than helped by it.

In retrospect, the most successful team members shared some common traits. They were mostly young—under 40. They remained positive and enthusiastic even during project travails. They were very agile, willing to change direction whenever the situation dictated. They were able to subordinate their personal and functional goals to the project's goal. They treated others on the project with respect and were not into blaming others when something went wrong. They were constantly learning and adapting their behavior as a result. They were willing to do anything to make the project successful, including working outside their functional area and working long days when necessary.

Terry Little's Key Traits of Successful Team Members

1. Young
2. Positive and enthusiastic
3. Agile; willing to change direction
4. Focused on the project goals over their own goals
5. Respectful of others; not quick to cast blame
6. Constantly learning
7. Willing to sacrifice for the project

I do not know how to identify people who will not work out with an interview; perhaps others are better at that than I am. What I do know is that poor performers disrupt team function and are intolerable over anything longer than a very short term. One of the project manager's most critical jobs is quelling those disruptive influences. [10]

Letting People Go

And sometimes, quelling disruptive influences means letting a team member go if his/her input is damaging teamwork and impeding progress. A manager needs to be aware, though, that such a decision may affect the team as a whole, and must therefore take steps to counter this possible impact. Katzenbach and Smith observe, "Theoretically, any time the membership of a team changes, the team itself has ended. ... Many teams, however, fail to think carefully about the transition caused by a change in membership" [11].

In the following case, Frank Snow, a Ground Project manager from NASA tried to deflate any bad feelings that might have otherwise surfaced when issuing a change in the team's membership, demonstrating his adherence to two major values: respect and adherence to tradition.

One member of the team was using "old school" methods that totally clashed with those of another team member who was working on the same simulation.

As Frank says, "I made the decision to let Mr. Old School go. I called him into my office and let him know that he was going to be reassigned to another project.

"My policy, however, was that when someone was leaving the project because of a personality conflict, everyone on the team, or as many of us who were around that day, went out for lunch as a send off. Sharing lunch together wasn't going to overcome the problems posed to the project by Mr. Old School, but if there was some bitterness—and sometimes there is—we were going to try to bury that and move on."

So Frank asked Mr. Old School where he wanted to have lunch. "He said, 'There's no reason to break with tradition. The Chinese place would be fine.' It was where we celebrated birthdays and project milestones, and indeed it was also the place to go when we needed to let someone go but wanted to soften any hard feelings ....

"We started off with tea and egg rolls, and by the time the lo mein got to the table, everyone was laughing and cracking jokes. Even though Mr. Old School and his counterpart couldn't agree on work, they had plenty to talk about. It turned out that they both had teenage daughters who were driving them crazy. In some ways, this is the kind of thing that can take the edge off of other differences. I could imagine them saying when they met each other again, in the cafeteria maybe, 'Hey, did that little girl of yours get her driver's license?' 'Yeah, and she's still driving me crazy, but how about you?' The best way to smooth out differences between team members is to give them a glimpse of one another as people outside of their work." [12]

Here, Frank Snow echoes Kevin Kelly's sentiment that the current economy "can only be built on relationships." It behooves managers to respect the humanity of their team members, rather than see them as cogs in a Taylor-esque "system." In his book, *Extreme Programming (XP) Explained*, Kent Beck, one of the leaders of agile software development, stresses that in addition to the four values of XP (communication, simplicity, feedback, and courage) there is one more overriding value: "a deeper value, one that lies below the surface of the other four—respect. If members of a team don't care about each other and what they are doing, XP is doomed." By showing respect to "Mr. Old School," Frank Snow undoubtedly reinforced this value within the team and successfully used the opportunity to enhance future teamwork [13].

The importance of Frank Snow's second value, adherence to tradition, is underscored by Bolman and Deal: "Ritual and ceremony are expressive activities. ... What transpires on the surface of such activities is not as important as the deeper communication underneath. Ritual and ceremony provide opportunities for reinforcing values, revitalizing spirit, and bonding individuals to the team and to one another" [14].

Critical Feedback

Letting people go is in fact a necessary step in some situations; however, at times it can be avoided when effective feedback is given to the team member. Research shows, however, that "Most managers hate giving critical feedback, and most employees detest receiving it" [15].

Terry Little shares with us a story about the dilemma of letting a person go or attempting to provide effective feedback:

I first met Dan when he came to my office to interview for a test engineer position on the project. An Air Force first lieutenant and Air Force Academy graduate, Dan was enthusiastic, positive, articulate, bright, humorous, self-assured, and extroverted. Even when I told him that I had very high expectations for every team member and would remove anyone who let the team down, he was confident that there would be no problem. We talked for about an hour and then I led him to the test manager's office for an interview; the test manager, Neil, would be his immediate supervisor. After Dan left, Neil gave me a thumbs up, but was a little concerned about Dan's youth and lack of experience. Dan would be the youngest person on the test team by far; he was in his early twenties and the next oldest test team member was more than 20 years older. I dismissed Neil's concern as overly cautious and resolved not only to hire Dan, but also to become his mentor.

I made it a point to talk with Dan almost every day during the first few months on the project. He was happy with the work and, importantly, Neil was very pleased with Dan's work on test plans and documentation. He seemed to fit well with the other team members and the fact that he was single with legions of girlfriends became a source of good-natured ribbing between the team members and Dan.

When the test team departed for a six-week stint at the test site I had no concerns about Dan. The test site was over 1000 miles away and I talked with Dan on the phone about once a week; everything seemed fine. Thus, after a successful test on a Friday, I was stunned to get a phone call from Neil when he told me that Dan had to go. He said that no one at the test site wanted to see Dan again. He started to tell me what Dan had done wrong, but I could tell he was fuming and sputtering. So, I cut him off telling him that we would talk about it face-to-face when he returned that evening.

It was about 7:00pm. I was sitting at my desk working when Neil came in. He angrily began to tell me about Dan's transgressions. Dan was a jerk. He was argumentative, he did not listen, he was always late to meetings, he disrespected the contractors, he did not follow directions and on and on. I listened without commenting. Then I said to him "Neil, this is what I want you to do over the weekend. I want you to give me 20 or so specific instances that include the context, what precisely Dan did or did not do and what the impact was on the team or mission. If it is too much to write down, use this voice recorder." I handed him a voice recorder. "Tell me," I said "what feedback did you give Dan?" Neil replied, "I have talked with him several times, but nothing has changed." "Ok," I said, "I will talk with Dan on Monday."

So, early Monday morning Neil presented me with a legal pad filled with detailed, numbered descriptions of what Dan had done. There were 35 instances over the six-week period. A few seemed minor to me, but most were not. I crossed through the minor ones and arranged the others from most to least significant.

I had set aside two hours that afternoon to talk with Dan. When he arrived he was his usual cheery self. I started off by asking him if Neil had talked with him about his behavior at the test site. Dan shook his head and said that he did not remember anything in particular. I told him that there were some issues and we needed to discuss them. So, I started down the list that Neil had given me. After the first one, I asked him what he had to say. "Nothing," he said. He gave the same answer after the second one and then the third one. I continued and he continued to indicate he had nothing to say. Finally, when I finished, I asked again what his response was. He looked down for about a minute in silence. I waited. He looked up directly into my eyes and said firmly, "I will change." That was that.

The whole one-way conversation had taken 30 minutes. As I reflected on the conversation, two things stood out. The first was that Dan did not try to deny or defend himself against Neil's assertions. Neither did he offer any excuses. He seemed to accept all of the accusations as true. The second puzzling thing was the disparity between Dan's recollection that Neil had never given him feedback and Neil's explanation that he had talked with Dan several times. After thinking for a while I concluded that both had been correct. Neil had thought he was giving feedback, but the casual manner in which he gave it was such that Dan considered Neil was simply making an offhand comment.

Feedback is indeed a gift—a rare one, unfortunately. My experience has been that most people who say they want feedback, really only want positive feedback—feedback that confirms the view they have of themselves. Very often these same people initially reject or ignore any feedback that might stimulate reflection or a behavior change. Bosses who should give feedback frequently do so in a sugarcoated way to minimize offense and conflict or, commonly, rationalize that giving feedback is useless. Many so-called "leaders" are conflict avoiders and only give "attaboy or attagirl" feedback. My belief is that giving timely effective feedback is the single most important thing a leader can do to mold an effective, learning, and vibrant team. My experience is that feedback improves performance at least 80% of the time. In fact, I have found that continuing feedback yields better teams than I have gotten when I have been able to hand select people. Certainly giving feedback is hard, but being a leader is hard. Moreover, a leader who cannot or will not give constructive feedback is not a leader. Now back to the story.

After my conversation with Dan, I went to see Neil and asked him to give Dan another chance. He reluctantly agreed after I told him that, if Dan misbehaved, he could send him back and I would remove him from the office. I also asked Neil to give me periodic reports on how Dan was doing.

Time went by. Dan and the team left for the test site. I anxiously waited for Neil's report on Dan's behavior, while I continued to touch base with Dan weekly. After about five weeks I got a call from Neil. He started the conversation off by saying, "I don't know what you told Dan, but it had an enormous impact; he has become a different person." He went on to sing accolades and praises for Dan and was emphatic about how valuable Dan had become to the team. Dan stayed on the test team for another year before he was promoted to and left for a new assignment. I remember Neil crying at Dan's going away party.

Twelve years later, I am in a different job in another building. I am sitting at my desk when the door opens and Dan walks in. He is dressed in a suit and his hair is longer. He tells me that he got out of the Air Force and then went to Yale Law School. He then began to work for a New York law firm and had recently become a partner. He had made a special trip to Florida to see me. We exchanged small talk and did some reminiscing about his time on the previous project. After about 30 minutes, he asks if he can get serious. I nod my head. He says, "I came here to tell you personally that you changed my life. Until you talked with me that day no one had ever been critical of me. I had thought I was perfect. I was insensitive to how my behavior affected others. I was arrogant and full of myself. I remember not saying anything to you during our conversation. That was because I was too shocked to respond, but I had enormous respect for you and had to accept the truth of what you were saying." With that, we shook hands and we left. Wow! Just wow.

» feedback is a means of respecting the individual

As this anecdote demonstrates, feedback is a means of respecting the individual and getting the most out of him or her. Due to Terry's feedback, Dan let go of his ego and became the right person for the job.

Focus on Team Collaboration

Once they have recruited the right people, successful project managers develop a collaborative team. They start by ensuring the development of an **interdependence-based** collaboration. Most of their efforts in building collaboration are usually spent on building trust among the various parties and individuals. Throughout the life of the project, however, they continue to engage in maintaining this collaboration [16, 17].

Interdependence-Based Collaboration

Most projects are characterized by an inherent incompatibility: The various parties executing the project are loosely coupled, whereas the tasks themselves are tightly coupled (see Fig. 5.2). When unexpected events affect one task, many other interdependent tasks may be quickly affected. Yet the direct responsibility for these tasks is distributed among the various loosely coupled parties, who are often unable to coordinate their actions and provide a timely response. Project success, therefore, requires the development of interdependence-based collaboration. The following story about Linda

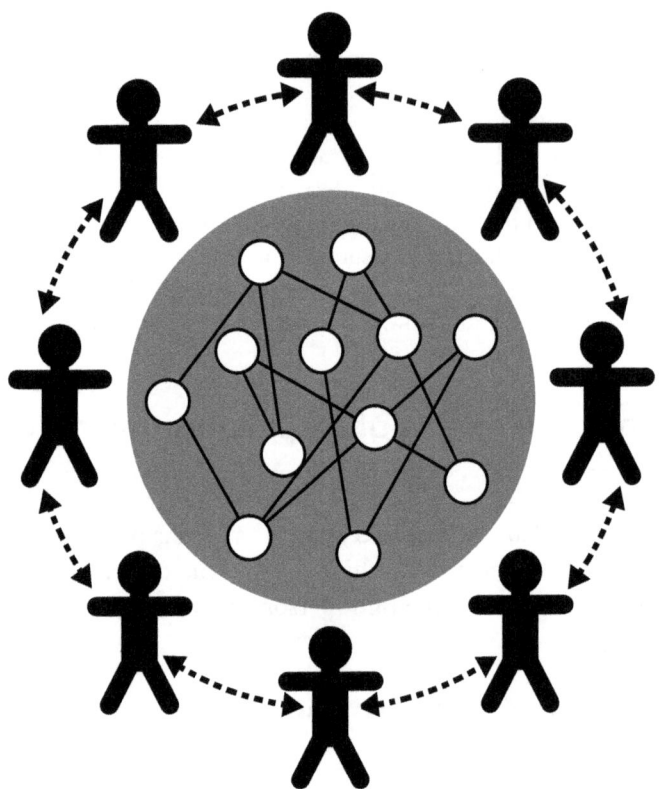

Fig. 5.2 The various parties executing the project are loosely coupled, whereas the tasks themselves are tightly coupled

Abbott, a Mission Business Manager from NASA, describes the development of a cross-disciplinary team which was better able to respond to unexpected events.

Space crafts are usually built with only a few large purchased items. Yet, they also have literally hundreds of small items that can make for the biggest headaches. It's something as small as a twenty-dollar connector that can halt integration, leading to a costly delay. After finishing the building of another spacecraft, it was clear to Linda that project success requires better collaboration, in particular between the technical and the procurement people.

Procurement's whole process is bound in rules and procedures, and is staffed by people that know the rules, but don't know about building spacecraft. ... Procurement works as a pool, with a first in, first out procedure. Generally, it works fairly well, and is actually relatively fair to all projects. But it's unable to respond to schedule-stopping unexpected events. The individuals in procurement see their job as procurement, not building spacecraft. They don't work with any one project closely enough to understand why that twenty-dollar connector is a multi-thousand-dollar emergency. Mostly, they don't have any personal investment in the project's success. It was important to get procurement on the team, rather than try to override them or work around them.

In order to circumvent the general pool procedure, Linda managed to convince procurement to assign two procurement officers to work exclusively on her project. The officers were integrated into the work of the team and invited to staff meetings. In the process of learning about the spacecraft project, they grew to understand why the technology was difficult and why unanticipated problems were inevitable, as well as the extent of their impact. Linda describes the gradual impact of one of the procurement officers who joined her team: "The more she learned about our project and worked on our team, the more she felt responsible for the project and wanted it to succeed. She found ways to expedite purchases when there were real emergencies. I can't tell you how many times she saved our bacon, times that were two days here, a week there, but that would have added up to a big, and costly schedule slip."

In turn, each of the team's engineers and scientists listened to the procurement officers, learning more about the procurement process and the 'why's' behind some of those pesky rules. As both sides came to understand each other's constraints, the interaction between them vastly improved, as did procurement's response to schedule-stopping unexpected events: "Together procurement became more responsive to our needs, and we became more responsible in meeting procurement's needs. ... By integrating them into the team, we changed an adversarial relationship into a group relationship. It became clear to all that 'if we fail, they fail.'" [18]

❯❯ No real teamwork can take place in an organization that maintains a traditional division of labor

The observation that "they don't have any personal investment in the project's success" most succinctly conveys why the structure of the traditional functional organization obstructs teamwork. No real teamwork can take place in an organization that maintains a traditional division of labor, given that the loyalties of the R&D, marketing, engineering, production, and procurement staff lie primarily with their respective disciplines, departments, and managers. Therefore, breaking down the organization's functional walls is the minimum requirement essential for teamwork.

However, integrating a group of people with a common assignment into an effective team may be even more difficult when the people in the group are affiliated with different organizations. This is illustrated in the next story told by Bill Clegern, a project manager from Procter & Gamble (P&G), who describes how a P&G resident engineer attempted to develop teamwork with his prime contractor:

> Pierre was the P&G resident engineer managing a major expansion at one of their plants in Europe. He was forced to work with Karl, the site manager from B&N, which was a highly reputable European contractor that won the bid for the facility work. Karl's workers had adopted a superior attitude toward all the other contractors on the site right from the start, and any team-building efforts by P&G were being undermined by B&N's incessant criticism of others and smug confidence about their own "professional" construction techniques.
>
> As Bill says, "Pierre ... grudgingly endured the situation, looking for an effective way to take Karl and B&N down a peg and get them on the team without damaging their effectiveness. Direct appeals to Karl, based on the premise that 'we're all in this together,' just didn't work. ... About three months into the job ... Karl discovered that one complete set of foundations on the south face of the facility's office expansion was located 30 cm inside the intended periphery. Over 200 lineal meters of strip foundations had just been poured in the wrong place. ... This was a serious mistake. ... Karl came, hat in hand, to Pierre to 'fess up ....'"
>
> Rather than demand that B&N start over, "Pierre immediately called a conference of the plant, engineering, and project leaders. [Together] they found a way to shift internal walls, realign halls, and adjust exterior windows in order to distribute the error without resulting in any functional or aesthetic losses. Although B&N's rework cost was considerable, it was far lower than that required for a complete fix and did not ruin the company's reputation. At the same time, P&G was able to stay on schedule without compromising the project's chance for success. Pierre did not take advantage of B&N nor kick Karl

'while he was down.'" The project was ultimately labeled a big success by all involved, and their new-found teamwork allowed B&N and P&G to collaborate on subsequent projects as well. [19]

»a group of people who do not feel dependent upon each other is a committee, not a team

---

These two stories—about Pierre and Linda—stress that unexpected problems are inevitable. When all project parties realize they cannot solve such problems alone, they embrace a philosophy of mutual interdependence and mutual responsibility for project results. Without such interdependence, project leaders must pay inordinate and unceasing attention to team maintenance. In essence, a group of people who do not feel dependent upon each other is a committee, not a team.

Trust

To create an effective team, it is not sufficient that the team members are aware of their mutual interdependence, they must also **trust** each other. In the following story, Frank Snow, the NASA Manager of the Ground System and Flight Operations, describes how he attempted to cope with the mistrust of his partner located about 2300 miles away from him:

> Frank figured the Flight Operations team, which he managed, should "get involved in the data analysis after launch, which was usually the sole responsibility of the science team." Frank's team knew the ground system well and Frank thought "they should, at the very least, train the people out at Caltech on how to use it." So he offered his help.
>
> According to Frank, "One of the Co-Investigators at Caltech, however, was terribly suspicious of the Goddard project office. Almost any help we offered to make his life easier was, he believed, a ruse to take control of his instrument. As appreciation for my offer, he sent me a blistering email that basically said, in 300 words no less, 'Hell no!' At that point, I decided to fly across the country to Caltech to talk with him. Maybe I'd have better luck in a face-to-face meeting."
>
> "I went there and listened to his concerns, I empathized with him, and then assured him that no one in the project office was trying to take anything away from him or from Caltech. In fact, we were actually interested in expanding Caltech's responsibilities, if they wanted this, to include flight operations. Moreover, I told him that I would put it into the operational plan to move the total operations of the spacecraft over to Caltech after launch."

"He never formally acknowledged it, but I think he saw that what we were offering was not such a bad idea after all. He allowed the Flight Ops team to come to Caltech and provide training in the ground system. … Clearly, face-to-face communication went a long way towards dispelling his suspicions about my intentions. I don't recall after this ever getting another 300-word email from him of the 'no-thank-you-and-please-go-away' variety. As a matter of fact, I think I could even say that this was the beginning of a fruitful relationship that lasted for the rest of the project." [20]

Face-to-Face

By taking the 2300-mile trip, necessary in this case for face-to-face communication, Frank Snow was able to change the mistrustful attitude of his co-investigator from Caltech. Indeed, face-to-face communication has several advantages over other forms of communication, rendering it a valuable tool for building trust. In contrast to interactions through other media that are largely sequential, face-to-face interaction makes it possible for two people to send and receive messages almost simultaneously. Furthermore, the structure of face-to-face interaction offers a valuable opportunity for interruption, repair, feedback, and learning that is virtually instantaneous. By seeing how others are responding to a verbal message even before it is complete, the speaker can alter it midstream in order to clarify it. The immediate feedback in face-to-face communication allows understanding to be checked, and interpretation to be corrected. Additionally, face-to-face communication captures the full spectrum of human interaction, allowing multiple cues to be observed simultaneously. It covers all the senses— sight, hearing, smell, taste, and touch—that provide the channels through which individuals receive information. Eye contact, body movements, and facial expressions may communicate a deeper meaning beyond the verbal message. For example, a sarcastic versus enthusiastic tone of voice adds essential meaning to verbal statements. Facial expressions usually communicate emotions, with the eyes expressing happiness, sadness, or surprise; and the lower face, brows, and forehead revealing anger. In one study of face-to-face communication, it was determined that only 7% of the content was transmitted verbally, whereas the remaining 93% of received information was contained in the tone of voice and facial expressions [21, 22] (Fig. 5.3).

Restructuring Relationships

Of course, rebuilding trust often requires more than just one face-to-face meeting. In the case of Judy Stokley, the project manager of the Advanced

Fig. 5.3 Face-to-face communication is critical: 93% of received information is contained in the tone of voice and facial expressions

Medium Range Air-to-Air Missile (AMRAAM) project of the US Air Force, the entire working relationship between the government and the contractors had to be restructured in order to make trust foundational to the collaboration.

> When Judy Stokley took over the Advanced Medium Range Air-to-Air Missile (AMRAAM) project of the US Air Force, the major development phases of the missile were over, and the project required primarily refinements and ongoing maintenance. The Pentagon decided it was time to cut down resources. However, as Judy discovered, not everyone at the Eglin Air Force Base in Florida was keen to change gears, and she faced strong opposition to changing the status quo. A great deal of ingenuity and stamina was required before she was able to achieve the needed reduction in resources, which included downsizing the engineering team from 80 to 12.
>
> Judy felt the time was ripe to propose similar downsizing to the two contractors responsible for the design, manufacturing, and maintenance of the missiles. However, it soon became very obvious to her that a radical shift in the organizational culture in both the government and in the industry was necessary, if any long lasting changes were to be implemented. The prevailing relationship between the two was basically deeply rooted mistrust. Government officials frequently expressed their belief that contractors would do anything to increase their profit as stated bluntly: "You can't trust these dirty contractors. They're all out to take advantage of you." On the other hand, the people on the

contractor's side believed that the Air Force team was willing to suck the company dry if that was what it took to get a low price. The result of this attitude was a complex and extremely wasteful system aimed at controlling everything the contractor set out to do. In turn, the government was expected to pay the contractor to make any change, or else it didn't get done. As Judy recalled: "If I want my contractor to flush the toilet in Tucson, I have to write him a contract letter and pay him to do it."

Judy set out to change the project culture, to create a relationship of trust, mutual support, and teamwork. As her first step, she hosted a meeting with several key leaders of Hughs and Raytheon, the program's contractors. Her first objective at the meeting was to underline what was wrong with their partnership. To make her point she presented a copy of the document that governed the project at the time. It included hundreds of pages outlining endless specifications as to the procedures necessary upon implementing any change. She wished to convince the contractors they should operate more independently, embracing a simple set of performance specifications that the contractor could control, trusting that the government would pay a fair price on the product. When she stated, "I am going to help you make a decent profit, and you are going to make sure that we have a good product out there," she believed they would take her at face value. But her first attempt at creating a true partnership failed miserably! As all of a sudden, Raytheon's chief engineer stood up and spoke across the room to his vice president: "Boss, I have got to make sure that before you agree to this, you understand what she's saying. … Today, if we change something here, the government pays; but what she's telling you with this deal, is that if we change something we pay!" The contractors were so cynical about working with the government that they had a hard time believing Judy could offer any kind of deal that would be good for them. It seemed that Judy had hit a dead-end.

Fortunately, the management philosophy of Chuck Anderson, the head of the AMRAAM project at Hughes, was much closer to Judy's than to his superiors in the company. In fact, he had demonstrated his approach in a previous interaction back when Judy served as Deputy Program Director. At the time, a design issue with the control section of the missile was uncovered. It was Chuck's second week on the job, when he went to Eglin Air Force Base and stunned the program director by stating he was going to fix the missiles at the company's expense. It was a $3-million decision, and the contractor was not obligated to fix the problem by any means. But Chuck believed that his company had a responsibility to take care of their customers and live up to their expectations.

When Judy took over as the project director, and Raytheon and Hughes were about to merge, Judy felt fortunate to have Chuck as the leader of the project following the merger, a teammate ready and willing to introduce reforms. A crucial meeting was held at the contractor's office, between the government's and contractor's staff, to lay out the foundations of a new agreement and to drastically reduce the number of contractor workers. They reached a stalemate. Finally, Judy and

Chuck stepped out to Chuck's office. They needed to decide how they were going to go about their business. They agreed the contractor would accept responsibility to do what was necessary and sufficient to develop, deliver, warrant, and support missiles that would be affordable, combat capable, and readily available. It meant eliminating the long waits required for government approval on changes the contractor felt were necessary. In layman's terms, it meant that the government would trust the contractor to decide when the product successfully met performance requirements. Judy went ahead and asked Chuck what he really needed to do the job. He said he thought he could downsize from 400 to about a hundred people. To seal the deal they simply shook hands!

Needless to say Chuck's team was shocked. They were aware that a handshake was the only assurance they had that the customer was going to live up to the agreement. But Chuck firmly believed that building trust between two parties begins by showing that you trust the other party. Yet, it was evident that intensive ongoing efforts were needed on both sides and at multiple managerial levels, in order to diffuse this situation.

Dennis Mallik, AMRAAM's Chief Financial Officer, was surprised to discover how little the contractor understood the Air Force's planning and budgeting procedures and constraints. He initiated a meeting to educate them regarding these issues. He discovered, for example, that the contractor's primary concern at the time was cash flow. The contractor people believed that if the Chief Financial Officer requested money one day it could be available the next day. They could not fathom that he had a two-year delay before he could get anything written into the budget! However, Dennis's understanding of the contractor's needs led to improving cash flow to the project. The visit netted a better rapport between the counterparts. They continued to meet face-to-face every couple of months, and maintained frequent e-mail and telephone communication on a regular basis.

But Dennis did not limit his communication with the contractor to educating him. He courageously developed an unconventional open relationship with Tom Gillman, the Contracting Officer for Raytheon. As reported by Tom, "It was the trust to be able to share with your counterpart what is really going on rather than some version that's been smoothed over by your leadership. It was the trust that your counterpart is going to listen to you thoughtfully and try to help you come up with a solution, but never use it against you. ... Dennis regarded me as a member of 'his' team as much as anybody who was in the room wearing a government badge. He asked me only once, 'Do you see anything limiting our abilities to get the job done?' After that, whenever I saw anything that could impact the AMRAAM project, it was expected that I would speak up and not wait to be asked for my input. It was all about our abilities to get the job done. I have to emphasize that word again: our." [23]

That's effective collaboration in a nutshell: when all team members refer to the project as "ours." Through mutual understanding and open communication, the AMRAAM project was able to ameliorate the culture of mistrust. In his *Harvard Business Review* article, "Trust and the Virtual Organization," Charles Handy asserts that it is more difficult to build trust in a virtual organization: "Trust is not blind. It is unwise to trust people whom you do not know well, whom you have not observed in action over time. … Trust needs bonding. … Trust needs touch. Visionary leaders, no matter how articulate, are not enough. A shared commitment still requires personal contact to make it real" [24].

To this end, Judy introduced "enablers," who were situated at the contractor's site:

This was the role of the Air Force "enablers" put on site to work side-by-side and support open communication with the contractor team members. Jon Westphal, an Engineer with the US, recalled his role as such an "enabler": "The first thing I had to do was try to convince the contractor that even though I was from the Air Force, I was there to help in whatever capacity I could. The contractor's employees wondered how safe it was to tell me anything and how much they should keep secret. I had to reassure them that whatever we talked about would remain confidential until we had identified the potential impact of the problem and created a plan to overcome it."

He further reported, "About nine months after I started going out to the contractor's site in Tucson, I needed to check something with the Director of Operations. I walked down to his office, where there were five or six engineers standing outside waiting in line. I walked up to the front of the line and was about to stick my head in the office and ask my question, when the guys in line jumped on me, 'Hey, what do you think you're doing?' I said, 'Look guys, I'm just going to ask Rick a quick question.' They objected, 'Come on now, there's a line here.' I said, 'Yeah, but I'm the customer.' And they said, 'You're an enabler. Get in the back of the line.' Right then, I knew that I had been genuinely accepted!"

The apprehension of the contractors from these implanted "enablers" was clearly described by Brock McCaman, Project Manager at Raytheon: "…These guys had complete exposure to all our dirty laundry. And I don't care how good you are, you still have some dirty laundry hanging around. I figured that this would be just another bunch of Air Force guys watching over us, reporting every little thing." But he admitted to being wrong, because under the leadership of Judy, reporting problems in the contractor's organization was considered as violating trust. The goal was rather to help solve the problems. Indeed, anytime a problem arose it was worked out before Air Force management even became aware of it.

At one point down the road, the contractor had a program-wide discussion about whether or not to continue using the enablers. Brock said, "Are you kidding? They're too valuable not to have around."

As summarized by Judy: "When you've got a strong trusting team, they will figure out how to overcome the little barriers that pop up along the way. By the second year, there were no barriers anymore. They did miraculous things, things no one would have believed they could do when we first started working together."

No doubt one of the major impacts of the new relationship between the parties was the contractor's enhanced sense of ownership and responsibility. This led, in turn, to multiple innovative initiatives resulting in significant improvements in performance combined with tremendous savings.

Brock McCaman recalled such an example. Traditionally, when a missile arrived at the contractor's depot, the clock started ticking, allowing the contractor exactly 60 days to do whatever was necessary to repair the missile and make it available for shipment. Sometimes a missile was returned so damaged that the contractor considered it "beyond economical repair." However, from the customer's point of view, everything was economical if you had already paid the contractor to do it. So the Air Force expected the contractor to return each damaged missile within 60 days, no matter what resources or efforts were needed to do so. Under the new arrangement, the contractor could decide what to work on and how to do so. Since a severely damaged missile was often followed by multiple missiles with minimal damage, the contractor could now complete repairing the less damaged missiles way ahead of the deadline. Thus, maintaining a much larger supply of missiles to the Air Force while significantly reducing the cost.

When the contractor assumes complete ownership he will go way beyond the contractual requirements. Tom Gillman recounted a case of how his people did just that. On a particular piece of missile hardware that had to work only 90 percent of the time, it was determined that failure occurred less than one percent of the time. Contractually, they were not required to resolve that one percent. Yet, they locked some engineers in the lab for six months and had them duplicate that failure. They ended up spending a couple of million dollars to fix 5,000 missiles that weren't under warranty. Nobody paid them to do the extra work, but it was the right thing to do for the war fighter.

At the end, the AMRAAM project received the DOD Life Cycle Cost Reduction Award. The average unit procurement cost for the project decreased from more than $750,000 to under $400,000, saving the Air Force and Navy $150 million over the course of four years. [23]

»when all team members have ownership, the product benefits

Clearly, trust was transformative for the AMRAAM project, showing that when all team members have ownership, the product benefits.

Maintaining Teamwork

Even when interdependence and trust between the various parties has been established, however, today's common and frequent unexpected events may negatively impact collaboration. Thus, throughout the life of the project, the project manager must be constantly ready to take action in order to maintain collaboration. This is how Allan Frandsen, a Payload Manager from California Institute of Technology, succinctly describes his rationale for **constant readiness**: "In running a project, I have always tried to anticipate problems. ... Despite your best-laid plans and ongoing attention to the job, the situation can turn to manure in a hurry if a personnel matter arises. So sustaining this prized team you have recruited has to be an important part of a manager's job" [25].

The following examples demonstrate how three project managers maintained teamwork. In the first example, Chuck Anderson, the Raytheon project manager of AMRAAM, shares a practice that he instituted to sustain the new relationships with the customer: stressing the **purpose** of the mission. Indeed, in a *Harvard Business Review* article, "Teamwork on the Fly," Amy Edmondson highlights the importance of emphasizing purpose: "Articulating what's at stake is a basic leadership tool ... it's particularly important in contexts that require teaming. ... Purpose ... can galvanize even the most diverse, amorphous team" [26].

> All 80 team members met once a month for half a day off-site at a hotel. They rented a ballroom, and the whole purpose of that meeting was to sustain the relationships with the customer and in particular, the mutual trust and strong commitment. It was to make sure that his team was constantly focused on the purpose of the project ... or brainwashed, as some said.
>
> During these meetings, Chuck encouraged open discussions with his team members, which did raise examples of how the Air Force wasn't living up to its end of the deal. But Chuck's message remained constant: "Let's try to work through this. ... Let's make sure that we deliver on time, make sure that the design is right, make sure that we meet every requirement. Our customer will help us in every way possible, and then by definition we'll succeed and we'll meet our financial targets." In essence, by constantly connecting his people to the purpose and to the mission of the project, he facilitated re-connecting them to the customer, and was able to maintain teamwork. [23]

Some patience and **tolerance for failure** can also be helpful in achieving the mission of the project, as exemplified in the JASSM case:

> By being a failure-tolerant leader, Terry Little, the JASSM project manager, was able to develop a culture of trust and commitment based collaboration. Larry Lawson, Lockheed's project manager, describes Terry's reaction to the team's initial failure and how he used it to help shape this culture: "After months of working seven-day weeks, our first missile launch after the contract award failed. ... It was the defining moment for the project. ... Terry could have said, 'I don't trust you, and I want to have an independent technical review.' But that's not what he said. ... Instead, he asked me if I wanted some help. Teams are defined by how they react in adversity—and how their leaders react. The lessons learned by this team about how to respond to adversity enabled us to solve bigger challenges." [27]

However, sustaining teamwork may also require radical steps that are very non-traditional. This is illustrated by Larry Goshorn, former Vice President of ITT Industries, who recounts the bizarre turning point in a project that was operating 300% over budget:

> Following a lot of finger-pointing and no real teamwork, there was a shake-up one day with the arrival of a new manager on the project who announced: "I just saw in the paper this morning that somebody has brought an elephant into town, and they're offering rides." Everybody else looked around the room, thinking, "Well, what has this got to do with anything?" And then the manager says to the other senior managers around the table, "Okay, you, you, you, and I are going to go over there, and we're going to ride this elephant."
>
> And there was great protesting. It seemed crazy. But, in the end, they went down the street a couple of blocks and rode this elephant. Believe it or not, from that point on, they started to cooperate a lot better. It's hard to argue with somebody that you've just seen hanging onto on the back of an elephant—especially when there are pictures.
>
> Goshorn concludes the story by reminding us that "you've got to do goofy things sometimes to get people to start working together" and "people working together is the only way to get out of a mess." [28]

There is a great deal of support in the literature for Goshorn's conclusion about doing silly things to bring people together. One of the steps proposed by Bolman and Deal for "making a team work" is to use **humor and play**: "Humor releases tension and resolves issues that arise from day-to-day routine or in a prevailing emergency. ... Work groups often focus single-mindedly on the task at hand, discouraging any unrelated activity. Seriousness replaces godliness as a desired virtue. Effective teams, on the other hand, balance seriousness with play and humor." Likewise, Jennifer James explains that "humor helps us deal with absurdities ... it renews energy and renews trust in ourselves, others, and the world" [14, 29].

The Keys to Building Trust

1. Interacting face to face
2. Restructuring to create mutual ownership
3. Stressing the purpose of the mission
4. Tolerating failure
5. Balancing seriousness with play

Develop and Sustain Teamwork by Focusing on the Work of the Team and Its Outcomes

Building teamwork by focusing on developing collaboration through interdependence and trust requires a supportive context and prolonged dedicated effort. However, developing teamwork can also be achieved when the work itself and its outcomes provide the stimuli for teamwork.

Katzenbach and Smith concluded in their highly acclaimed book *The Wisdom of Teams: Creating the High-Performance Organization*, "A demanding performance challenge tends to create a team. The hunger for performance is far more important to team success than team-building exercises" [30].

Similarly, a recent *Harvard Business Review* article argued that "Culture isn't something you 'fix.' Rather ... cultural change is what you get after you've put new processes or structures in place to tackle tough business challenges. ... The culture evolves as you do that important work" [31].

The following case study, which describes the design and construction of a very large dairy, will demonstrate how teamwork can be developed and sustained by focusing on the work of the team and its outcomes.

Tnuva Food Industries Ltd., a 70-year-old company and one of the ten largest industrial companies in Israel, initiated a major organizational change. No longer would each of five small local dairies produce and market all of its dairy products to the local buyers. Rather, three large, modern dairies would be built, each with its own production specialty, relying on logistics centers for distribution. One of these three new dairies was slated to specialize in cup products (cottage cheese, yogurt, etc.). The constructed facility would cover about 60,000 square meters with the equipment linked together by more than 80 kilometers of stainless steel pipe and 7,000 automated valves. It was expected to be the largest dairy in the Middle East and among the largest ones in Europe.

Two major groups of engineers were to be engaged in the engineering and construction work required for the plant. The construction group was responsible for the design of the building and its systems, including air conditioning, refrigeration, electricity, communications, water, sewer, and outdoor development. The equipment and processes group was responsible for designing the production and transportation equipment and for arranging it in the optimal way. While the construction engineers and architects were almost all local, all the equipment and processes engineering was done outside Israel, mostly in Germany (primarily by GEA).

Following a thorough selection process, Zvika, a senior manager from a large project management company, was hired by Tnuva to lead the planning and construction of their new dairy. During his first months on the job, the dairy project was forced to adapt to three distinct overriding strategies. It started with the development of a state-of-the-art-driven dairy, a "dairy of dreams" as they termed it. When they found that this strategy led to a huge growth in project scope and overall cost, they embraced a "cost-driven" orientation. Yet, when Tnuva's upper management learned that their domination in the dairy cup products field was about to be threatened by their greatest rival, they switched one more time, this time to a "schedule-driven" focus. Each change of strategy meant major adjustments.

Thus, a few months into the project, the equipment and processes design was still in its infancy, and it was clear that GEA was not ready even with the preliminary equipment plans. As these plans were to determine the dimensions and requirements of the facility, Tnuva could not fulfill its contractual obligation to provide the construction designers with the basic data needed to begin designing the structures. Furthermore, it seemed that too many functionaries at Tnuva as well as at GEA still did not feel the pressure to move forward. Many issues were continuously debated as if constant delays and stalemates were just unavoidable. By that time, Zvika realized that probably the only two key people who were really concerned about the constantly delayed timetable were Ofer, the CEO of the dairy division of Tnuva, and Zvika himself. Being a very experienced project manager, Zvika thought that despite the lack of information from the German designers, it was time to move ahead with planning and construction. He believed that prolonged delays at this early stage would only legitimize further delays. Moreover, he was of the opinion that starting before all open issues are resolved is the best way to ensure their speedy resolution necessary to maintain forward momentum. He came to the conclusion that a radical step was necessary.

Zvika called for a meeting. Tnuva's equipment and process people strongly recommended that the design and construction of the facilities not be allowed to start for at least six more months, by which time they claimed all the needed information would be available from GEA. Zvika made it clear that due to the upcoming wet winter season, a 6-month delay would automatically lead to at least a 12-month delay. It was clear that the project could not wait one full year. While decoupling the construction component of the project from the equipment and processes component was expected to be costly, Ofer, the CEO of the dairy division, declared that in order to meet the necessary timetable, he was ready to bear the consequences of starting construction prior to finalizing equipment planning. At last, the project was about to shift gears from park to drive.

While agreeing to proceed with construction, Tnuva's officials believed they could continue with their common practice of issuing a bid and signing a contract with one large construction firm. However, Zvika was adamantly against this approach. He believed that since the project was huge, complex, and schedule-driven, it was necessary to develop a construction organization which was highly adaptable and responsive and which would be able to cope with numerous delays and changes. Convincing Tnuva's management to abandon the standard process, he not only split the work to multiple contractors, but also significantly shortened the time necessary to select them by moving the process to the construction site and by streamlining it. For the most part, he selected people that he knew from his own past experience to be competent, trustful and, most of all, responsive. In the interests of enhancing responsiveness, Zvika primarily recruited designers with offices in the vicinity of the project so that frequent visits to the site would not be a problem. During the negotiations, Tnuva went along with Zvika and kept the price level fair and often favorable to the designers, thereby enabling them to demand a particularly high quality of service.

At this point Zvika recruited Mike, a 69-year-old civil engineer, as the person who would serve as the overall manager of construction. While he knew that Mike had vast experience working on large and complex projects, he was concerned as Mike was rumored to have a "centralist" personality, with trouble accepting authority. He feared their personalities may clash. They agreed to a mutual trial period of three months, during which they would try to define the appropriate "division of labor" between the two of them.

During that time, because of the slow and unpredictable flow of basic information from GEA, the design of the facility was not smooth. In spite of the burden resulting from the need to coordinate between many contractors, they split the project among a large number of contractors. At the peak of operations, there were around 250 different contractors and suppliers in construction alone. For example, there were ten contractors simultaneously working on the concrete skeleton, another eight on the steel frame, six in stainless steel, and another four on electrical systems. Zvika and Mike took advantage of the situation, as it allowed them to create competition between the contractors. Each contractor who completed his work to their satisfaction immediately received another "chunk of work." Mike made sure to keep continuity by providing the contractors with work in order to avoid wasting equipment and manpower.

Indeed, Mike was a man of extremes. He helped in every possible way the contractors that he considered to be good, while he did not hide his dislike towards those he considered inferior. When the manager of a certain contracting company came on site in fancy clothing or in a Mercedes, it drove Mike crazy. As much as he could, he made sure that those contractors would not work again in his territory. Mike was also a man of action who hated sitting at large meetings, which he viewed as an outrageous waste of time. He preferred to focus on helping the contractors on site. He loved meeting and talking "on the scaffolding" with work managers as well as with the "simple" workers. The contractors loved him and trusted him blindfolded, knowing that he would not hold back any effort to help them with anything. Thus, for example, if one of the contractors had trouble with cash flow, Mike would convince Tnuva to pay a one-time sum as a premium beyond the contract, which would allow the contractor to complete the work in the meantime. At the end of the three-month trial period, there was no question in Zvika's mind as to whether Mike would be staying. Their strong cooperation had surprised both, and they knew that it was a great success not only for them, but for the project itself.

Both Zvika and Mike considered excellent communication between everyone involved in the construction to be of outmost importance for accelerating construction. To encourage ongoing planning and coordination among all the design engineers, and to ensure that all designers in Israel and in Germany were working with the most up-to-date version of the plans, they put a unique intranet system in place. The system allowed everyone to view and use all the plans in the system in real time. Furthermore, they installed an advanced work station on site to produce blueprints. The blueprints were sent to the site via the intranet, and within minutes, all the necessary copies could be made and distributed to the many contractors on site. In addition, the team of twelve inspectors on site carried out daily documentation of progress via digital cameras to be distributed via the intranet network to all the designers and contractors in Israel and abroad. The construction site was even photographed once a month from the air, with the most recent photographs compared with the photographs from the previous month and sent to all managers at Tnuva and GEA. By displaying the monthly progress in a clear and vivid way, Zvika was trying to call everybody's attention to the fast progress on site, and especially to convince GEA that it was time to accelerate their pace of work.

Zvika summed up his team's approach: "As much as we invested in 'high-tech' communication, I believe that the key was rather 'high-touch' communication and especially being 'close to the action' on site." Therefore, all project meetings, from the beginning of the work to its end, took place on site. For this purpose, Tnuva built a temporary, but comfortable and sophisticated, office building on site. The designers of the facility met weekly there, and each of the meetings began with a tour of the site. These meetings were very effective, both for solving problems in real time and for building strong cooperation among the various design engineers. The best example of how rich and frequent face-to-face communication can connect people and make them into a cohesive team was the daily meetings that Mike held with his team of twelve inspectors whose expected role was to continuously verify that the work was being performed according to the project design and specifications and the accepted standards. As elaborated by Mike: "Each one of the inspectors undertook a specific aspect of the project, and in that framework acted relatively independently, felt responsible for it, and was committed to its success. Each day the entire team gathered to analyze the contractors' performance, to share learning, and to prepare for the next day. The intensity of performance and the daily meetings created a 'team spirit,' extending to informal meetings, held even outside of work hours and including other family members, which contributed greatly to strengthening the connections made during work."

Gradually, under Mike's leadership, a harmonious relationship developed between the inspectors and the contractors. Mike made the inspectors see the contractors as their customers and perceive their job as helping the contractor produce quality work, as if they were his consultant or partner rather than his policeman. Rather than wait until a problem developed and became visible and difficult to rectify, the inspectors together with the contractors solved problems as soon as they arose. In this way, the unpleasant control function of the inspectors became a very productive joint problem-solving function. In Zvika's opinion, this unexpected role of the inspectors was probably the most crucial factor contributing to the quality, efficiency, and speed of the project's execution. [32]

Reflecting on the project and on the impact of Mike's leadership several years after project completion, Zvika felt that both groups, the inspectors and the contractors, were highly motivated because of the job itself, the work and its ongoing outcomes. Indeed, Bennis and Biederman, who studied the work of very successful groups, provided the following explanation for this phenomenon: "Great work is its own reward. Great groups are engaged in solving hard, meaningful problems. ... Given a task they believe in and a chance to do it well, they will work tirelessly for no more reward than the one they give themselves" [33].

As time went on, the friction between GEA and Tnuva and the on-site construction team did not subside. GEA was very busy with other projects in Europe and chose to match the pace of their work to the premise that the construction team would not be able to complete and hand over the structures for equipment installation according to the planned schedule. Suddenly, they realized that their assumption was wrong. Construction was about to be completed, and GEA—still hopelessly behind schedule—was going to be held responsible for the delays.

The CEO of the dairy division decided it was time for a reality check and an ultimatum. In a stormy meeting held in Germany with GEA management, he complained about their great delay and threatened that if the size of their design team was not increased significantly and immediately, Tnuva would fine them for damages. As recalled by the CEO: "I specifically referred to the milk basement, which GEA had promised to begin working on in two months. The CEO of GEA was astounded that I dared claim that the completed basement would be handed over to GEA at that time, when two weeks earlier he had been informed by on-site delegates that the basement floor had just been poured. I immediately called Zvika and asked him to photograph the status of that day and send it to me by email. The photograph showed that during those two weeks, the basement foundation had been entirely completed. ... It seemed to me that my visit put GEA under great stress because their premise that the facility would be delayed had not stood up to the test of reality."

The GEA installation teams, including about 35 people, arrived at the site as agreed. The disputes between GEA and Tnuva continued. This time, GEA needed Tnuva's approval for changes to already constructed facilities, such as cutting large openings in existing walls. These proposed alterations would be very costly, both in terms of money and time, and this added friction was not helpful for progress on site.

However, Mike was able to smooth things over. The fact that he was also American and was fluent in many languages, including English and German, was a big advantage in this project, which involved working together with many foreign companies and experts from a wide variety of countries. As it turned out, speaking German became crucial when GEA arrived on the scene. Mike had cultivated an overall friendly working relationship with the GEA on-site manager. At the end of each work day, the two had developed a habit of meeting in the office for a glass of whisky; when all the troubles of the day were brought up, issues that needed coordination were pinpointed, and a work plan for the following day was agreed upon. The two had a liking for "betting" on tasks that seemed impossible, and the loser had to pay for drinks that day. This informal relationship helped substantially in reducing the stress between the two sides. As recalled by the local project manager for equipment and processes: "Mike helped me a lot in dealing with the German contractors. He developed very unique ties with them, and they trusted him much more than they trusted the Tnuva people. He won their highest level of cooperation."

Zvika summarized Mike's crucial role to the success of the project: "The dairy project required me to make more than a few difficult decisions, which led me to take several out-of-the-ordinary actions. Looking back at the project, I think that the most unusual action, and the most successful one, was creating the role for the general contractor and recruiting Mike for the job. Mike and I are such different people, and yet, we were able to easily split the work between the two of us and to cooperate in the most harmonious way possible at all the times. I believe the key was that Mike is a person who does what he says, a person you can easily trust. You can quickly gain his trust if you happen to belong to the camp of people who do what they say they would. Having Mike on the team allowed me to concentrate on planning and preparing for the next month and the next quarter, knowing that today and next week are being taken care of by him in the best possible way." [32]

»If I had to choose the one motivating factor that seems to me to be operating in most successful people, it would be the wish 'to make things happen

---

Mike's behavior can probably be explained nicely by the following Edward de Bono statement: "If I had to choose the one motivating factor that seems to me to be operating in most successful people, it is the wish 'to make things happen'" [34].

This feeling of cooperation and mutual respect was expressed in the "Holiday of Holidays" event. When Mike learned that in December, the holidays for the Jews (Chanuka), the Muslims (Eid al-Adha), and the Christians (Christmas) were set to fall during the same week, he decided that this was an excellent opportunity to celebrate and to say a loud and clear thank-you to all 500 workers on site. He declared that pouring the second concrete ceiling, which had been done around the same time, and which was completed faster than expected, was a good enough reason to throw a joint party for all the workers. The event was nicely organized and was funded by Tnuva and the various contractors, and included a personal gift that was distributed to all of the workers. A nice printed card was attached with a message in three languages (Hebrew, Arabic, and English), in which Tnuva thanked the workers for their contribution and wished them a happy holiday. Outside catering was ordered, and nice tables with food and drink "fit for a king" were set up and served personally to all the workers by the catering staff. All the contractors were asked to arrive that day in festive clothing, and the CEOs of all the companies as well as from Tnuva also attended. Workers and exceptional contractors received certificates of appreciation. The event aroused a lot of excitement and pride.

Upon project completion, Tnuva was extremely satisfied with the results, most importantly, with delivering the project on time. [32]

It is clear that the two leaders of the construction component of the dairy project, Zvika and Mike, appreciated the importance of teamwork, and were able to develop and sustain it. Yet, throughout the life of the project, they always focused first on maintaining project progress, and they hardly dedicated specific time and resources for building collaborative teamwork. At the same time, very often they were able to design the organization of the work in a way that promoted collaboration, and to utilize the progress of the work to harness and sustain this collaboration.

So how does one build and sustain teamwork? Is it by focusing directly on the collaborative work of the team (as discussed in the previous section) or by focusing on the work of the team and its outcomes (as discussed in the current section)? In *The Soul of a New Machine*, Tracy Kidder presents examples of developing and sustaining teamwork through both collaboration-oriented steps as well as through challenging and meaningful work. Indeed, in most projects, developing and sustaining teamwork is achieved through a combination of the two approaches. As Katzenbach and Smith conclude, "In the final analysis, performance is both the cause and effect of teams" [35, 36].

Gardener: The Fourth Role of the Project Manager

In recent years the concept of gardening has been advocated by many experts as a suitable metaphor for developing and sustaining teamwork. Like project team leaders, who must take an active role in ensuring productive interdependence and collaboration within their teams, gardeners must also manage the interactions among their plants. Not unlike people, different plants possess different attributes. Thus, they may provide support for each other, as seen, for example, when herbs confuse insects with their strong odors, acting as repellents that mask the scent of the would-be host plant. On the other hand,

Fig. 5.4 Like a gardener, project managers looking to get the most from collaboration must choose the right plants for the "job" and must pay attention to how the plants coexist with one another

plants may actively compete with other plants for space, or even poison their neighbors' offspring to maintain a competitive advantage.

Likewise, project managers looking to get the most from collaboration must choose the right plants for the "job" and must pay attention to how the plants coexist with one another. As succinctly described in a recent blog regarding leadership: "We create the right growing conditions, nurture healthy soil, plant a diverse variety of sturdy, healthy plants that co-exist, and watch them grow. We adjust as we go along, removing excess weeds, mulching, preventing insects, watering and fertilizing. ... Gardens need constant tending" [37] (Fig. 5.4).

Blending the Four Practices of the Project Manager: Planning, Agility, Resilience, and Collaboration

---

» the effective implementation of each practice requires the support of other practices

---

This fourth role, gardener, is performed alongside the project manager's other three roles, discussed earlier: decision choreographer, plumber, and entrepreneur (see Fig. 5.5). These roles each rely on a different practice—planning, agility, resilience, and collaboration—presented in separate chapters as stand-

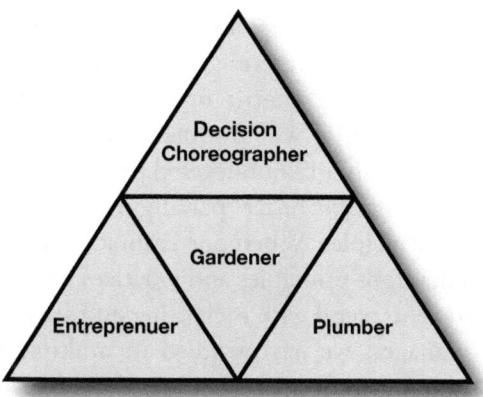

Fig. 5.5 The four roles of the project manager

alone practices. Yet, it bears repeating that the practices are interdependent; the effective implementation of each practice requires the support of other practices.

Thus, for example, the development of the elaborate project collaborations described in the current chapter, were enabled by the *resilience* of leaders who were willing to challenge the status quo. In the AMRAAM case, for instance, the government and the contractor were able to develop strong collaboration only because their two respective leaders, Judy and Chuck, were willing to challenge the existing norms in their organizations. Similarly, in the dairy case, Zvika and Mike enabled the building of collaborative teams by taking multiple nonconformist steps while *planning* and organizing the work on site.

Chapter 3 explained how the second practice (responsive agility) continuously supports the first practice (evolving planning). Indeed, successful project managers strive to minimize the negative impact of the unexpected events by being quick to respond (agility) in order to be able to regain project stability as soon as possible and restart work according to the project plans. By employing the agility approach, they can quickly rely again on the planning approach.

Furthermore, throughout the book we provided multiple illustrations showing that today's project managers have to periodically cope with deviations from the plans (the focus of the first practice), to continuously cope with unexpected events (the focus of the second practice), and to occasionally cope with major threats (the focus of the third practice). We also highlighted that the difficulties in coping with these three types of changes are exacerbated by the fact that project organizations are composed of heterogeneous units. The overall purpose of the fourth practice, developing and maintaining collaborative teamwork, is to facilitate the implementations of the first three practices and thus cope most effectively with project changes.

In Chap. 1, we shared the concept first introduced by the French Nobel Prize winner Henri Bergson that there is no such thing as disorder. Instead, there are two sorts of order: geometric order and living order. We further explained that in today's world, where projects have to cope with multiple changes and problems, one should not develop principles based on theoretical studies relying on the "geometric order" paradigm. These studies will typically produce independent principles. When one embraces the "living order" paradigm, however, and develops principles and practices based on "real life" projects, the practices prove to blend with each other and are interdependent. The successful project managers we have studied in multiple field studies have repeatedly demonstrated the effective blending of the four practices.

Key Points

- Collaboration differentiates successful projects from unsuccessful ones.
- People are the "make or break factor" for success, but stars aren't necessarily the right people.
- It always pays to treat the whole team with respect; tradition and critical feedback can aid in bringing about that respect.
- Creating a truly cross-disciplinary team is often more effective than maintaining a traditional division of labor.
- Teams function best when they're truly interdependent and when there's mutual trust.
- Trust can be maintained through face-to-face interaction, restructuring relationships, and maintaining teamwork by emphasizing purpose, tolerating failure, and using humor and play.
- Challenging and meaningful work can itself create meaningful collaboration, especially when team members are united by the "wish to make things happen."
- The fourth role of the project manager is as a gardener, tending to the culture of the garden, pulling weeds, positioning plants to the best mutual effect.
- The four roles of the project manager are interdependent.

References

1. Kanigel, R. *The One Best Way: Frederick Winslow Taylor and the Enigma of Efficiency*. 1997, New York: Viking Penguin.
2. Kelly, K. *New Rules for the New Economy: 10 Radical Strategies for a Connected World*. 1999, New York: Penguin: p. 118–39.

3. Flores, T. Earthly Considerations on Mars. *Ask Magazine* 2003; 51: p. 5–8.

4. Collins, J. *Good to Great: Why Some Companies Make the Leap... and Others Don't*. 2001, New York: HarperCollins: p. 13.

5. Kilts, J.M., Manfredi, J.F., and Lorber, R. *Doing What Matters: How to Get Results that Make a Difference: The Revolutionary Old-school Approach*. 2007, New York: Crown Business: p. 146.

6. Schwer, K. Start up. *Ask Magazine* 2003; 11: p. 18–20.

7. Colvin, G. Why Dream Teams Fail. *Fortune* 2006; 153(11): p. 87–92.

8. Berkun, S. *Teams and Stars*. 2005: http://scottberkun.com/essays/47-teams-and-stars/.

9. Snow, F. Give It to Chuck. *Ask Magazine,* 2003; 11: p. 12–13.

10. Laufer, A. and Russell, J. First Who...Then What. *Consortium of Project Leadership*. http://living-order.blogspot.co.il/2016/04/first-whothen-what.html. April 2016.

11. Katzenbach, J.R. and Smith, D.K. *The Wisdom of Teams: Creating the High-Performance Organization*. 1993, Boston, MA: Harvard Business Press: p. 164–5.

12. Snow, F. Tried and True, in *Shared Voyage: Learning and Unlearning from Remarkable Projects*, A. Laufer, T. Post, and E.J. Hoffman, Editors. 2005, Washington, DC: The NASA History Series: p. 62–3.

13. Beck, K. *Extreme Programming Explained: Embrace Change*. 1999, Boston, MA: Addison-Wesley Professional: p. 34–5.

14. Bolman, L.G. and Deal, T.E. What Makes a Team Work? *Organizational Dynamics* 1992; 21(2): p. 34–44.

15. Cannon, M.D. and Witherspoon, R. Actionable Feedback: Unlocking the Power of Learning and Performance Improvement. *The Academy of Management Executive* 2005; 19(2): p. 120–134.

16. Baker, D.P., Day, R., and Salas, E. Teamwork as an Essential Component of High-Reliability Organizations. *Health Services Research* 2006; 41(4): p. 1576–1598.

17. Styhre, A. Leadership as Muddling Through: Site Managers in the Construction Industry, in *The Work of Managers: Towards a Practice Theory of Management*, S. Tengblad, Editor. 2012, Oxford: Oxford University Press: p. 131–145.

18. Abbot, L.F. Teaming to Make a Routine of the Impossible, in *Project Management Success Stories: Lessons of Project Leaders*, A. Laufer and E.J. Hoffman, Editors. 2000, New York: John Wiley & Sons: p. 158–162.

19. Laufer, A. *Simultaneous Management: Managing Projects in a Dynamic Environment*. 1997, New York: AMACOM, American Management Association: p. 144–5.

20. Snow, F. Small Wins Make for Big Gains, in *Shared Voyage: Learning and Unlearning from Remarkable Projects*, A. Laufer, T. Post, and E.J. Hoffman, Editors. 2005, Washington, DC: The NASA History Series: p. 53–54.

21. Landau, M. Redundancy, Rationality, and the Problem of Duplication and Overlap. *Public Administration Review* 1969; 29(4): p. 346–358.

22. Mehrabian, A. *Silent Messages*. 1971, Belmont, CA: Wadsworth.

23. Laufer, A. *Mastering the Leadership Role in Project Management Practices that Deliver Remarkable Results*. 2012, New Jersey: FT Press: p. 125–147.

24. Handy, C. Trust and the Virtual Organization. *Harvard Business Review* 1995; 73(3): p. 40–50.
25. Frandsen, A. Project Management: Easy as ABC, in *Shared Voyage: Learning and Unlearning from Remarkable Projects*, A. Laufer, T. Post, and E.J. Hoffman, Editors. 2005, Washington, DC: The NASA History Series: p. 47–9.
26. Edmondson, A.C. Teamwork on the Fly. *Harvard Business Review* 2012; 90(4): p. 72–80.
27. Laufer, A. *Mastering the Leadership Role in Project Management Practices that Deliver Remarkable Results.* 2012, New Jersey: FT Press: p. 49.
28. Goshorn, L. Pulling Stories Out of the Trunk. *Ask Magazine* 2003; 15: p. 15.
29. James, J. *Thinking in the Future Tense: Leadership Skills for a New Age.* 1996, New York: Simon & Schuster: p. 175.
30. Katzenbach, J.R. and Smith, D.K. *The Wisdom of Teams: Creating the High-Performance Organization.* 1993, Boston, MA: Harvard Business Press: p. 3.
31. Lorsch, J.W. and McTague, E. Culture Is Not the Culprit. *Harvard Business Review* 2016; 94(4): p. 96–105.
32. Laufer, A. *Mastering the Leadership Role in Project Management Practices that Deliver Remarkable Results.* 2012, New Jersey: FT Press: p. 193–211.
33. Bennis, W. and Biederman, P.W. *Organizing Genius: The Secret of Creative Collaboration.* 1997, Reading MA: Addison-Wesley: p. 215.
34. De Bono, E. Tactics: *The Art and Science of Success.* 1984, Boston, MA: Little Brown and Company: p. 54.
35. Kidder, T. *The Soul of a New Machine.* 2011, Boston, MA: Back Bay Books.
36. Katzenbach, J.R. and Smith, D.K. *The Wisdom of Teams: Creating the High-Performance Organization.* 1993, Boston, MA: Harvard Business Press: p. 107.
37. *Gardening Is The Best Metaphor For Leadership. ONPOINTLEADERSHIP;* http://www.onpoint-leadership.com/2014/06/gardening-is-the-best-metaphor-for-leadership/.

6

Becoming a Project Leader: Learn on the Job Through Experience, Reflection, and Mentoring

"Leadership, like swimming, cannot be learned by reading about it."
Henry Mintzberg

The large sample of project managers we studied did not become successful due to intensive and formal classroom education. Rather, the primary means for their development was on-the-job learning. In this chapter we will introduce three avenues for on-the-job learning which we have found to be effective in many of the organizations we studied. The first entails exposing the project manager to multiple diverse experiences and challenges, the second involves the process of mentoring, and the third consists of learning through communities of practice.

Pursuing Challenging Tasks

As early as in 1989, Lombardo and Eichinger at the Center for Creative Leadership, an institution founded to advance the understanding, practice, and development of leadership, published a short book titled *Eighty-Eight Assignments for Development in Place* [1]. The book is in line with Ashby's law of requisite variety that proclaims that "only variety can absorb variety" [2]. This well-known law of cybernetics asserts that the greater the variety of actions available to a control system, the greater the variety of perturbations it is able to compensate. In other words, a system cannot meet increasing variety

© The Author(s) 2018
A. Laufer et al., *Becoming a Project Leader*,
https://doi.org/10.1007/978-3-319-66724-9_6

in its environment unless it increases the range of its response repertoire. Carrying out multiple different tasks increases the potential repertoire for developing managers to cope with a large variety of challenges.

» the impact of the task on personal development is related to the degree to which the task is challenging

While such developmental tasks can vary from assignments such as handling a negotiation with a new customer or installing a new system, to managing different groups of individuals such as peers or experts, the impact of the task on personal development is related to the degree to which the task is challenging [1]. Moreover, successful project leaders develop by initiating unique actions which challenge the status quo. Following are three examples of actions taken by a project manager early in his career that marked his development as a project leader.

Roy, a young captain in the Engineering Corps of the Israeli Defense Forces, recounts some of his most impactful on-the-job learning experiences. Note that in each case, Roy met the challenge by seeking a solution he would have been unlikely to have learned in a formal training program.

Admitting Mistakes and Changing the Organization's Practices

In the first case, Roy was in charge of a project involving the design and implementation of a new road reaching the top of a mountain 700 yards high, where a new intelligence base was to be constructed in a very short time prior to the retreat of Israeli forces from the Suez Canal.

Roy's team, which consisted of three civilian engineers hired to design the road and prepare the bidding documents, estimated the cost of the road at 1.6 million dollars. The bid was won by a contractor whose estimate was 1.4 million dollars. However, in spite of the fact that the project was completed ahead of time, the actual final cost was 2.2 million dollars! Roy and his civilian engineering team were baffled.

Roy decided to consult an old friend of his, a very experienced retired contractor. It took his friend 15 minutes to study the documents before he burst out laughing. Roy had apparently been a victim of an old trick of road contractors. The design of an uphill road requires estimating what percent of the way will require simple inexpensive support to establish a stable road and what percent will require building very expensive retaining support walls. In this case the contractor during his initial onsite visit estimated that at least 60% of the road would require expensive retaining walls, while the inexperienced design engineers estimated that only 10% of the way would involve such walls. The winning contractor therefore submitted a relatively low price estimate for the unsupported portion of the road while at the same time significantly increasing the price estimate of the support walls. Since the contractor's estimate was more realistic (60%), his profits were accordingly much higher. Needless to say, from that point forward, Roy became much more vigilant about contractor estimates. But he went a step further: he told others about his mistake. He made sure his superiors as well as his colleagues learned of his misadventure, and in doing so, saved much money and grief for the years to come. His efforts to make sure the insights he gained became common knowledge led to fundamental changes in the practices of the entire organization regarding hiring consulting engineers.

Combining Work for Different Clients

In his work in IDF, Roy could hire the design engineers directly, although he was not responsible for paying them. All the work with the contractors was conducted through civilians in the Department of Defense (DOD). The rationale was to decouple the army officers from any direct interaction with money exchange to ensure transactions were not affected by bribery.

Once a month, the regional director at the DOD invited Roy and his 12 colleagues to meet and discuss events related to their work in the recent and upcoming months. At the end of the two-hour meetings, all participants usually left, except for Roy who often stayed behind to chat some more at the request of the director. In one of these informal one-on-one meetings, the director raised a major concern. He told Roy that while reviewing the various bids submitted in recent months, one factor had become obvious. Because of the pressure due to the impending withdrawal from Sinai, many of the submitted bids were for very small projects, such as a small medical center at a cost of $200,000. Apparently, small and less qualified contractors are more apt to submit bids for small jobs. The unit cost for these small jobs was much higher than the unit cost of larger jobs. Upon Roy's request, the director shared with him his data supporting this claim.

Roy used this information to argue with his supervisors that projects for serving different customers (e.g., Intelligence, Communication, Airforce), traditionally handled by different engineering units, should be combined. This was an unprecedented proposal. Yet, using the data from DOD, Roy was able to convince the chain of command to change the traditional work groups, resulting in significant cost reductions.

Stalling a Project

Colonel J., commander-in-chief of the Engineering Corps, had an open door on Mondays at 7 PM for all captains and majors in his units. Very few utilized this after-hours opportunity. Roy was the exception. In one of their meetings, the colonel confided in Roy that a senior major in Roy's unit was about to leave the unit in three weeks. The colonel suspected that the major was trying to funnel a major contract to a friend of his. There was no hard evidence, but both the colonel and Roy agreed that this contractor was not the best one for the job. Roy used every trick in (and out of) the book to stall the progress of the bid: he raised questions that required preliminary investigations; he presented past examples which indicated the need to investigate the specific contractor more thoroughly; and at the end he even took some 'sick leave' which delayed major meetings regarding the selection of the contractor. But it was for the good of the project, the military unit, and the client. His efforts were successful in delaying the final decision regarding the selection of the contractor [3].

» taking initiative while consistently challenging the status quo is one of the key ingredients in developing leadership competence

---

All three episodes presented obstacles—either in the form of failures or threats. In each case Roy chose to challenge the status quo and offer innovative solutions, knowing that acting out of the box may have increased the risk of failure. Nevertheless, Roy was resilient and continued to constantly seek ways to improve his projects and the function of his organization. These three episodes demonstrate why Roy became known over the years as one the best project managers in the IDF corps of engineers. They highlight that taking initiative while consistently challenging the status quo is one of the key ingredients in developing leadership competence.

Mentoring

Mentor, in Greek mythology, was the name of a wise advisor to Odysseus, entrusted with the teaching of Odysseus' son, Telemachus. Through Mentor's guidance Telemachus became an effective and loved ruler. Mentoring, at the most basic level, is simply the act of helping another person learn and is the most natural way for developing young project managers on the job. While mutual trust is the foundation of the relationship between the mentor and mentee, to make a positive lasting difference on the attitudes, knowledge, skills, and prospects of the mentee, the mentor must develop a variety of skills and assume a range of roles: he must be a model to be emulated, an expert and advocate providing advice and feedback, and a friend.

» the key to successful mentoring is the ability to adapt the relationship to the needs of the mentee

---

Much has been written in recent years regarding mentoring in management in general, but that literature doesn't address project management [4–6]. In this brief section we do not attempt to provide a detailed outline of the roles and skills necessary for effective mentoring, nor a guideline as to how to develop these skills. Rather we have chosen to present the reflections of two successful project managers: the first, by Jason Kruger from Boldt, who had limited experience as a mentor; and the second by Terry Little from the Air Force (a coauthor of this book), who is a very seasoned mentor. These stories, written by individuals from completely different backgrounds and work experiences, demonstrate that the key to successful mentoring is the ability to adapt the relationship to the needs of the mentee.

Learning to Step Aside
By Jason Kruger, a senior project manager from Boldt Construction Company

My role within the company changed [when I became a senior project manager]. I had to focus my efforts on developing and mentoring people versus managing the day-to-day details of a project. One of the challenges of this new role arose with an individual whom for this story we'll call Mack.

Last year, Mack had a tough year. In my opinion, he had a lot of the qualities of a leader that we look for, but his performance was inconsistent. Mack was unreliable, his communication was poor, he struggled to stay on top of his projects, and he had challenges working with the subcontractors and other Boldt team members. Mack was working on several large remodel projects I had developed with a client who had grown to trust Boldt and particularly me. Mack understood the client's relationship with me, and relied on me for some of the tougher decisions, and he pulled me in to meetings with the client. I must admit, I loved getting into the details of the project and solving the issues. But I also was concerned because I felt Mack was relying on me too much.

In a review with my supervisor, we decided to give Mack one more shot to prove he could fit in with the team and perform at a high level. My supervisor charged me with handling Mack's review and having the difficult discussion with him. We were going to put him on a new project as the site project manager, but if he did not perform consistently at a high level, we were going to have to part ways. On the other hand, if he performed well, we would promote him to Project Manager and continue to develop his career.

I had a very tough conversation with Mack. He was surprised, not at his performance issues (we had discussed similar things several times in the past) but because I was telling him it might lead to him being let go. We worked on a plan for his development together and over the course of the following weeks, we had a lot of difficult conversations about performance, expectations, improvement, and leadership.

When the new project began, the situation did not improve. The project was developing quickly and we were nearing the start of the installations, but with Mack's performance thus far, I had to have another conversation with my supervisor. I didn't think it was going to work out. This time, my supervisor looked at me and asked what I had done differently to change my approach with Mack. I didn't expect that. He asked what I was doing differently in my mentoring and communication to get Mack to learn differently. Then he explained it to me with a simple analogy. He told me I had developed into a position of leadership because of my success in the past. I had acquired my own trophies and placed them in my trophy case. As a result, I was given more leadership opportunities. In order for me to continue to grow in my leadership role, I had to let others acquire trophies for their trophy case and feel success or failure. I had to let them develop their own style as I had, and let others gain recognition for their efforts. I had to stop being so protective. He also told me to read a book he was reading called *The Servant: A Simple Story about the True Essence of Leadership*. I read the book and considered our conversation. It was one of those major "Aha!" moments in my life. I was suffocating Mack by trying to get him to do things the way I did them, using the same tools, managing the same way. I was also solving all of Mack's issues for him because of my fear of letting him fail. Without knowing it, I was stepping into his limelight every time senior management came around, and he was in my shadow (Fig. 6.1).

So I changed my style with Mack. When he had issues, I asked questions to get him to come to a resolution on his own. I stayed away from the project when others visited. When I was asked to give a presentation on what we were doing, I let him give it and receive the accolades. I changed my communication style with him.

The results were tremendous. He showed incredible growth since his review. He gained more self-confidence, knew his projects inside and out, developed strong relationships at multiple levels, and started to mentor his project team members. He became one of our stronger young leaders and we promoted him to project manager.

Fig. 6.1 Is the trophy case yours or your mentee's?

I still struggle with the balance of managing the details and stepping aside to let others lead in their own way with some guidance. But I continue to work on it and to mentor with the philosophy "Let others put trophies in their trophy case." I learned that I need to understand more about my team members and flex my leadership style to better fit each of my team members [7].

Jason discovered something crucial for effective mentorship: the mentee must be allowed to own his successes and failures. It can be difficult to let go, given the personal investment that many mentors have in their mentees, but it's essential for growth.

Meaningful Mentorship
By Terry Little, from the US Air Force

No one that I know in a senior position got there without some mentoring along the way. Usually they've had informal mentoring, and usually it started early in the career with more than a single mentor. But there are many different ways to get the benefit of mentoring. It can be done in a way that is formal, informal, or in a way I like to call "informal-informal."

Formal Mentoring

》 Many so-called leaders fail to recognize that mentoring is as important as anything they do and more important than most of what they do

---

It's been my experience that formal mentoring programs almost never work, and there are varying reasons for this. One is that such formal programs demand a pervasive management commitment across an organization that almost never exists. Second, many senior people give mentoring lip service but are unwilling to spend the time that it takes to do it. Notice I said unwilling rather than unable. Many so-called leaders fail to recognize that mentoring is as important as anything they do and more important than most of what they do.

The third reason formal programs fail is that they are incentivized by external reward rather than a desire to improve and grow. Would-be mentees clamor to become a part of a formal mentor program, just so they can add it to a resume. This leads, in turn, to a bureaucratic selection process where paper matters more than real accomplishment. The truth is that many people can derive no benefit from mentoring because they think they already have all the answers, because they have limited potential, or because they view mentoring as just a way to get a better job with higher pay. Mentoring needs to be selective.

Informal Mentoring

My strong preference is for informal mentoring; I want to pick whom I mentor. For instance, in my current job I have selected seven people within the Agency. How did I select them? I used my own observations, and the opinions of others whom I respect, to identify mid-level project managers with high potential to become senior managers. Only one of those people actually works for me and there are two that I frankly don't like very much. That's OK because not all high-potential people work for me or are to my liking. And why did I choose mid-level managers instead of junior-level managers, who might be in their more formative years? The answer is two-fold. Number one, mentoring takes a lot of time and effort, and I have limited time and energy. I would rather do a reasonable job mentoring a few than a pitiful job mentoring many. Number two, mentoring is everyone's responsibility and not just the responsibility of those in senior positions. Put another way, every mid-level manager has an affirmative responsibility to mentor those below him or her in the pecking order. Part of my role in a senior position is to communicate my expectation to those below me that they have a mentoring responsibility for which I hold them accountable.

So how do I do my informal mentoring? I meet with each person I mentor regularly—nominally once a quarter. I also meet with everyone I mentor as a group once each six months. In between, I send articles or suggested readings, as well as some words of counsel that come to me. To me and to them it's critical that these things be predictable and personal—something they can count on and that means something to them as diverse individuals.

When we recently met as a group, we discussed the importance of maintaining unbridled passion about our work, while avoiding counterproductive displays of emotion. We tried to come to grips with how to maintain our dignity and grace in the face of adversity. We also addressed the importance of focusing on the job-after-next as a guide star for deciding what to do now. In the cases of the individual meetings, I typically answer any questions and give direct feedback on areas where each person may need improvement. For instance, I told one individual recently that his manner of dress (casual, with a short sleeve shirt, no tie and relatively disheveled hair) impacted his ability to influence people and left a bad first impression. He argued that his manner of dress shouldn't matter. I countered that whether it should or shouldn't matter is irrelevant. It does and he should do something about it if he wants to lead. I told another person that she did too much talking when she should be listening. I gave her several examples. Both people thanked me for the feedback and related that no one had ever given them such constructive feedback in their entire careers. Perhaps it was easier for me to do this since neither of the people worked for me, but I think it's a pretty sad commentary that neither of them had ever had the benefit of the most basic mentoring tool: timely, constructive feedback.

Informal-Informal Mentoring

Finally, my favorite mentoring is what I call "informal-informal" mentoring. I like it because it's unconscious and natural for the mentor (especially valuable for a lazy one like me) and because those getting the mentoring don't even know that it is happening. As we progress up the career chain, our behaviors become more and more visible to an increasingly larger number of people. We are not conscious of it, but others take their cues from those higher up the bureaucratic pyramid than they are. They observe our behavior and make judgments about it. Is it something worth emulating? If so, how can I adapt that behavior to my unique personality? Is it something to avoid? If so, how do I sensitize myself so that I don't do it unconsciously? Much of what we turn out to be as individuals derives from what we have learned from observing others—not from what others have told us, what we have read and so forth. When others seek to emulate us, we have mentoring at its finest. Each person may have his or her own style that precludes direct "copycatting." But when one sees basic leadership principles working effectively in real life, it can have a profound effect [8].

Terry Little's Lessons on Mentoring

1. Mentors must be willing to spend time doing it
2. Mentees must be willing to learn
3. Mentoring is everyone's responsibility, not just the responsibility of those in senior positions
4. Advice to mentees should be predictable and personal
5. With any position you hold, your behavior should be worthy of emulation

Both Jason and Terry stress two key points. First, working with the guidance of a mentor is crucial for the development of the project manager. Second, while informal mentoring is generally more effective than formal mentoring, it must be tailored to the needs and learning style of the individual. At the end of the day the mentor often benefits from the process no less than the mentee, and therefore it is strongly recommended that all project managers engage in mentoring not only to advance the function of the mentee and the organization but also as a means for self-development.

Learning Through Stories in Communities of Practice

"Communities of practice" is a term used to describe groups of people sharing a common interest, craft, profession, or passion, who interact on a regular basis in order to learn and improve their abilities. Although the phenomenon of engaging in a process of collective learning is long-standing and includes activities such as students learning together for exams or artists meeting regularly to discuss painting techniques, it was Lave and Wenger in their 1991 book *Situated Learning* who first coined the phrase "communities of practice" [9]. Whereas communities of practice can take many forms, they all share three key features: (1) the community members are brought together by a common learning need; (2) the shared learning experience creates between the participants a long-lasting bond; and (3) the shared interactions affect their practice (Fig. 6.2).

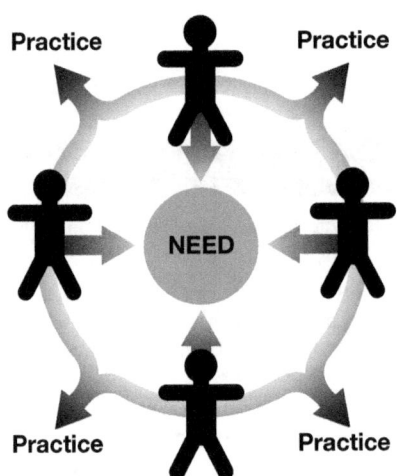

Fig. 6.2 The three key features of communities of practice: NEED brings people together; a BOND is formed; the interactions affect PRACTICE

Over the years we, the authors, have used communities of practice as a means for developing project managers in numerous companies such as Procter & Gamble, Motorola, NASA, and Skanska. We used personal stories shared by the participants as the key activity during the community of practice meetings. In this final section, we will illuminate the power of storytelling in developing and transferring knowledge, and we will provide guidelines for writing effective stories. We will then present general guidelines for establishing a central, ongoing, and structured community of practice. We will end with stories demonstrating the benefits of using the principles of community of practice in workshops delivered throughout an organization to promote organizational learning and to develop the competence of its practitioners.

The Power of Stories

In his capacity as a consultant for Procter & Gamble (P&G), Alexander Laufer accidentally encountered stories as a possible tool for uncovering and formulating project management knowledge:

》stories have unique power, not only for sharing knowledge but also for generating new knowledge

---

During my third visit to Procter and Gamble (P&G) I realized that the conventional mode of consulting was insufficient for the quick, wide, and lasting assimilation that was essential for developing organizational knowledge and competent project managers.

My answer to this problem was storytelling. Why? I realized that people's minds are changed more through observation than through argument. I therefore thought that the telling of real-life stories by credible and successful managers, colleagues from their own company, would serve as an efficient substitute for observation.

The results of my effort at P&G exceeded my wildest expectations. At the conclusion of a workshop where project managers presented and discussed their stories, Mr. Denker, a senior manager at P&G, commented, "I would never have believed that such a profound change in language, focus of attention, and way of thinking could have taken place within a two-year period."

For me personally, however, the most unexpected and lasting result of using stories at P&G was realizing that stories have unique power, not only for sharing knowledge but also for generating new knowledge. As a researcher, I found that this was indeed a very effective way to learn from practitioners. [10]

Alexander Laufer's research projects produced more than 700 stories collected from more than 200 competent practitioners, which led eventually to the publication of five books [11–15].

Why are stories so effective for generating project management knowledge? Project management lies somewhere between a "technology" and a "craft," though probably closer to a craft (see Fig. 6.3). Project managers are not like laboratory technicians or bookkeepers, who have highly structured practices and procedures which can be completely described and taught with the aid of formal rules. Such technical knowledge is sometimes called "explicit"; it's accessible to people other than the individuals originating it. But neither is project management like skilled trades, such as bricklaying and carpentry, which are acquired mainly through demonstration and apprenticeship, and which rely more on "tacit" knowledge—semiconscious and unconscious knowledge stored in the minds of individuals rather than codified in a manual. While some aspects of project management knowledge are explicit, a great deal of it, especially in a dynamic, complex, and fast-changing environment, is tacit. Based on a variety of sources regarding ways for capturing tacit knowledge, there is ample evidence to support the view that a good story is often the best way to convey meaningful (tacit) knowledge [16, 17].

❯❯ Happenings become experiences when they are digested, when they are reflected on

---

Stories are also excellent tools for enhancing reflection [18]. In his book, *Managers Not MBAs*, Mintzberg stresses that "Activity becomes 'experience' only after it has been reflected on thoroughly" [19]. He cites T.S. Eliot,

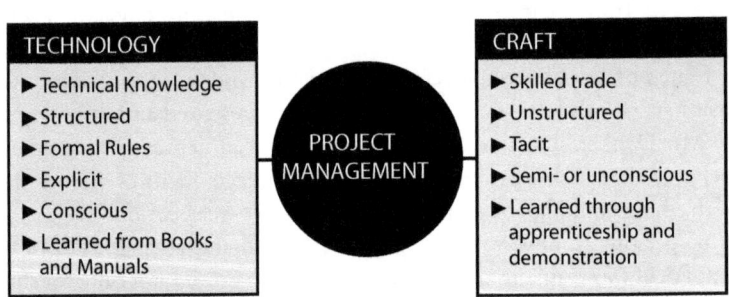

Fig. 6.3 Project management lies somewhere between a "Technology" and a "Craft"

who wrote in one of his poems, "We had the experience but missed the meaning." He also cites Saul Alinsky, who argues that "Most people do not accumulate a body of experience. Most people go through life undergoing a series of happenings, which pass through their systems undigested. Happenings become experiences when they are digested, when they are reflected on, related to general patterns, and synthesized." In recent years, many leading organizations have started using stories to capture and disseminate knowledge, in particular when attempting to create a "learning organization" [20, 21].

However, organizations may sometimes find they need to change a culture or a mindset rather than just educate. Such unlearning is also aided by stories. As Nisbett and Ross suggest, people are more inclined to change their mindset on the basis of vivid information. They explain that information is considered vivid when it is emotionally interesting, concrete, and imagery-provoking [22]. Good real-life stories told by successful and credible managers usually convey vivid information and thus may facilitate changing a mindset.

How to Write a Good Story

People love to read stories because they attract and captivate, can convey a rich message in a non-threatening manner, and are memorable. Stories are thus the most effective learning tool at our disposal, especially in situations where the prospective learner suffers from a lack of time—which is the case for most project managers. What follows is a brief guide (from Laufer and Hoffman's *Project Management Success Stories: Lessons of Project Leaders*) [23] for writing an effective story to share in a community of practice.

What is a story? In its broadest sense, a story is an account of actions in a time sequence; plot orders the actions and brings causality to the events. Good stories make us want to know what happens next. They introduce a conflict or a problem to be solved, bring us to a point of crisis, and then present the solution to the problem. The best ones build suspense and excitement as they go on, and very often use every day, conversational language, the language you might use when talking to a friend.

What isn't a story? It's not a report or a summary; it isn't filled with headings, or bar charts, or graphs; and it isn't a philosophy, although stories can often be used to illustrate one.

What stories are worth telling? Those that share something important to you, that carry a lesson you think others should hear.

What doesn't belong in a story? First of all, untruths. Although fudging a bit to emphasize a point might not hurt, if you stray too far from the truth, your story loses credibility. Also, too many (or too few) details don't belong. You should keep the story simple and short—and focused on a single event—while still giving your reader enough detail to understand.

How do I get started? Remember that the story begins as a draft only. You don't have to get it right the first time, or even the fifth. You can revise. You might try telling the story to someone else before you actually write it down, just to get your storytelling juices flowing. Once you're ready to start writing, an outline might help you include everything in the story that is necessary. Try the following:

1. **Title**. Begin with a title if you have one. However, it isn't necessary for getting started. Often it is easier to find a title after you have completed the writing. Your title should tell the reader what your story is about. Try to find a clever and meaningful phrase—this will help capture your reader's attention.
2. **Context of the Story**. Tell the reader the specific circumstances and environment of the story. Include your relationship to the events. This sets the stage for your story.
3. **The Problem**. Because you don't want to lose your reader with too many details, move quickly to the problem. Explain the issue that had to be resolved and what caused it to be a problem in the first place.
4. **Possible Solutions and the One Selected**. If you can, tell the reader what other solutions you rejected and why, as well as what caused you to choose your solution. The rationale behind the chosen solution, as well as why you rejected the alternatives, can be very beneficial information for the reader. Keep in mind, too, that you should be presenting a unique solution, something you yourself didn't anticipate and that others likely would not have anticipated.
5. **The Consequences**. Tell the reader the result of implementing the solution you chose. What happened when you did what you did?
6. **Conclusion**. Tell the reader what you learned from this experience. Although you should avoid being too didactic, you do want to be certain that your story's message is clear. The whole point of sharing stories in a community of practice is to illuminate some basic truth that others might find educational.

Building Communities of Practice

What follows is a model for building a community of practice, used by the authors with great success at companies like Procter and Gamble (1991–1994), Motorola (1995–1996), the US government (1998–1999), NASA and the US Airforce (2000–2005), Skanska and Turner (2006–2008), and Boldt (2011–2015). The communities of practice created in these organizations maintained activities over periods of years, and the majority of the stories presented throughout this book were generated in these forums. Following is a general guideline used by the authors to establish the communities of practice:

1. **Forum Selection.** The best project managers in the organization are identified by their management and selected to serve as the community of practice forum. In large corporations, about 50 project managers may serve in the forum. Senior management is excluded from the meetings.
2. **Forum Meetings.** Typically, the forum meets twice a year for 2.5 days per meeting, or four times a year for 1.5 days per meeting.
3. **Selection of Executive Committee.** At the first forum meeting, a committee of three project managers is selected to manage the activities of each meeting.
4. **Generation of Stories.** Prior to each meeting, each member of the forum is requested to submit a story to the executive committee. At the initial forum meeting, it may be helpful to examine some already-written stories for the dual purpose of discussing their insights and how to write an effective story. The forum may ask for a practice or a tool instead of a story.
5. **Story Selection.** The committee, together with two senior managers from the company, selects several stories (usually between 8 and 10) from those sent in for the next forum meeting.
6. **Deliberations During the Meetings.** During the next forum meeting, the stories are told by their authors and discussed and reflected upon, first in small groups and then by the entire forum. Through such discussions tacit knowledge of the story teller is converted to explicit knowledge shared by the entire forum.
7. **Story Revision.** As a result of the individual reflections and community discussions, the stories are revised by their authors.
8. **Story Publication.** The stories are then published and shared with the entire organization.

While the presented model has been shown to be very effective in developing the competence of project managers as well as in transferring important knowledge throughout the organization, it no doubt entails a serious investment on the part of the individual sparing the time for lengthy meetings, as well as on the part of the organization allocating the resources for these meetings.

Over the years we have witnessed adaptations to this comprehensive model. While these adaptations may not capture all the benefits of ongoing communities of practice forums, by emulating some basic features of our model, primarily the use of stories to reflect upon and share individual experiences, they have been very successful in helping develop competence in the practitioners as well as the transfer of knowledge throughout the organization.

» Step away from your work for a moment to better understand it, learn from it, and then share what you learned with others

One such adaptation was developed by Denise Lee who was at the time a member of the team headed by Alexander Laufer organizing the central community of practice at NASA. While this very successful community of practice met many of NASA's needs, Denise felt that it was important to help cultivate a culture of on-the-job knowledge sharing also among NASA's practitioners who were not members of the community of practice and were located at NASA centers throughout the United States. As stated by Denise, "Our aim was to help the men and women who work on NASA projects step away from their work for a moment in order to better understand it, learn from it, and then share what they learned with others" [24].

To this effect she created the Transfer Wisdom Workshops to be held at various NASA Centers. Her idea was to recruit to the workshops not only project managers or even people on a project management career track. She targeted people from the different disciplines contributing to the project, trying to get them to embrace the philosophy of knowledge sharing and put to use some of its practices. The beginning was slow, as she had to sell her idea at the different centers. However, through active recruiting and word of mouth, the workshops grew from merely five participants in the first center to over 25 participants in subsequent workshops.

The process of the workshop was described by Denise as follows:

We began with some stories from ASK Magazine [NASA's knowledge-sharing publication, which presented stories from NASA's community of practice] as a starting point, asking people to read the stories and then talk with the small groups we had set up. Slowly, as people finished reading, we heard the murmuring of conversations. Soon, the entire room was discussing the stories and leveraging the knowledge in the stories to talk about their own work. Lessons were continuously being generated and shared, generated and shared. ...

... They left feeling that they had spent their time productively and had learned a great deal from one another. [24]

Following are two stories that arose from Denise's Transfer Wisdom Workshops at different NASA centers. Note how each story lays out its context, problem, solution, and lesson.

Trusting the Enemy
By Terri Rodgers, John Glenn Research Center

The opportunity to manage a flight project came up, and I was eager to see what that world was like—to actually see hardware fly. The only catch was that the opening occurred because the current project manager wanted out. It was too much work on top of his other workload, and the project scientist was driving him crazy.

Sure enough, as soon as I took the job, the project scientist started complaining all the way up to his management chain. We would be in a meeting and have to step outside to argue over some disagreement. Finally, I decided, "If you can't beat 'em, join 'em." I started to listen closely to his concerns and realized that some were valid. I also started to recognize his strengths, and I capitalized on them. He was quite articulate, and he was willing to share his ideas with an audience. I asked him to present a few charts at our monthly presentation to management. I also included him on the telecoms with our payload support managers at Marshall Space Flight Center and Johnson Space Center. These simple things gave him more insight into what was going on with the project, and they cost me nothing.

The project moved along and before too long our hardware was tested and ready to fly. It was time to present our work to management during a two-day review. The project scientist faded into the background because he trusted me to do my job. The first part went fine. I went home Friday evening, thinking about what I would say on Monday. But things didn't work out the way I planned. I was eight months pregnant, and I went into premature labor. I called work to say that I wouldn't be in on Monday.

When Monday came, the project scientist did a wonderful job presenting my charts—but not before praising me for the job I had done. This from a person who looked more like an enemy than a friend when I first met him. You can go far when you reach out to "enemies" and listen [25].

Get in Bed

By Jon Bauschlicher, Kennedy Space Center

During a long and checkered professional career, I was taught to "never get in bed with the customer." While working for the government (NASA and US Air Force), "getting in bed" with the customer/supplier would, at worst, compromise your objectivity and result in a conflict of interest, and, at best, give the appearance of impropriety.

While working in private industry, we were told that "getting in bed" with the customer/supplier would reveal minor flaws in your product or process that the customer didn't really need to know about. We were told that the customer would nitpick you to death with questions and concerns that weren't important, and that decision-making would be delayed by bringing someone else into the decision-making process. We were told that proprietary products or design processes would be revealed to someone without a "need-to-know."

One project changed my feelings about all that. Project KAFFU (Kiwi Air Force Fighter Upgrade) was a fighter retrofit program for the Royal New Zealand Air Force; we were trying to give F-16 capabilities to old A-4 fighter aircraft. When the contractor I was working for won the competition, the contract included sharing office space with the Royal New Zealand Air Force engineers, pilots, and maintainers throughout the entire development, prototype, and flight test effort—cradle-to-grave, as far as the engineering effort was concerned.

We sat side-by-side with these guys. They participated in every facet of the engineering development program. They helped write requirements, software, drawings, specifications, test plans, test procedures, and test reports. They worked in the lab integrating and testing hardware and software. They knew how things worked, and they saw things fail. They saw smart and dumb engineers and managers. They worked and played with all of us. Aside from a few classified areas, they had full access to our entire facility—our engineering labs, work areas, and our cafeteria.

They were truly, fully, integrated into our engineering team. And the results?

We had product advocates (the Royal New Zealand Air Force engineers) who were trusted by both the customer (the Royal New Zealand Air Force) and the supplier (us). With less engineering work for us, we produced a product that more fully addressed our customer's needs and requirements. It was a better product—more capable and user-oriented—than we would have produced without the active participation of the customer's engineers, operators, and maintainers. And, in the end, we had a well-informed, well-educated customer expert in our system's uses and capabilities.

Overall, the results from "getting in bed" with the customer were nothing like I had been taught they would be. Nothing but good came from the effort, and both customer and supplier benefited—the ultimate win/win situation [26].

Meaningful Growth

We opened the chapter with Ashby's Law of requisite variety: "only variety can absorb variety." Project managers develop as successful leaders by employing a variety of practices which are from bottom to top (the project manager tackling challenging tasks and affecting the organization), top to bottom (mentoring), and across the organization (community of practice) (see Fig. 6.4). If an organization is to grow and weather the inevitable ups and downs it will face in a dynamic environment, professional development is essential. The tried-and-tested practices described here all but guarantee meaningful growth.

Key Points

- Project managers learn the most when they seek challenges and respond to those challenges in unique ways.
- The key to successful mentoring is the ability to adapt the relationship to the needs of the mentee.
- Communities of practice consist of people brought together by a common learning need.
- Stories help COP members bond and are key in transferring knowledge.
- Experience becomes meaningful after it's reflected upon.
- Meaningful on-the-job learning arises when people know how to tell stories and how to build effective communities of practice.
- If an organization is to grow and weather the inevitable ups and downs it will face in a dynamic environment, professional development is essential.

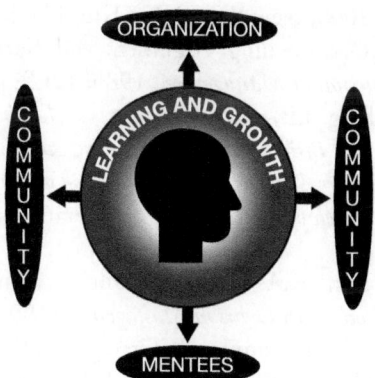

Fig. 6.4 The successful leader's matrix of meaningful growth

References

1. Lombardo, M.M. and Eichinger, R.W. *Eighty-Eight Assignments for Development in Place*. 1989, Greensboro, North Carolina: Center for Creative Leadership.
2. Ashby, W.R. *An Introduction to Cybernetics*. 1956, London: Chapman & Hall.
3. Roy, L., interviewed by Alex Laufer. 2011. (November).
4. Bell, C.R. and Goldsmith, M. *Managers as Mentors: Building Partnerships for Learning*. 2013, San Francisco, CA: Berrett-Koehler Publishers.
5. Peddy, S. *The Art of Mentoring: Lead, Follow and Get Out of the Way*. 1998, Houston, Texas: Bullion-Books.
6. Shea, G.F. *Mentoring: A Practical Guide*. 1997, Menlo Park, CA: Crisp Publications.
7. Kruger, J. *Learning to Step Aside*. Presentation, Boldt Semi-Annual Community of Practice Meeting, Nov. 2014.
8. Little, T. "Meaningful Mentorship." *Ask Magazine* 2004; 19: pp. 20–21.
9. Lave, J. and Wenger, E. *Situated Learning: Legitimate Peripheral Participation*. 1991, Cambridge: Cambridge University Press.
10. Laufer, A. *Simultaneous Management: Managing Projects in a Dynamic Environment*. 1997, New York: AMACOM, American Management Association: p. 5.
11. Laufer, A. *Simultaneous Management: Managing Projects in a Dynamic Environment*. 1997, New York: AMACOM, American Management Association.
12. Laufer, A. and Hoffman, E.J. *Project Management Success Stories: Lessons of Project Leaders*. 2000, New York, NY: Wiley & Sons.
13. Laufer, A., Post, T., and Hoffman, E.J. *Shared Voyage: Learning and Unlearning from Remarkable Projects*. 2005, Washington, DC: The NASA History Series.
14. Laufer, A. *Breaking the Code of Project Management*. 2009, New York, NY: Palgrave Macmillan.
15. Laufer, A. *Mastering the Leadership Role in Project Management Practices that Deliver Remarkable Results*. 2012, New Jersey: FT Press.
16. Mintzberg, H. Developing Theory about the Development of Theory, in *Great Minds in Management: The Process of Theory Development*, K.G. Smith and M.A. Hitt, Editors. 2005, New York, NY: Oxford University Press.
17. Weick, K.E. and L.D. Browning, Argument and Narration in Organizational Communication. *Journal of Management* 1986; 12(2): p. 243–259.
18. Jalongo, M.R., Isenberg, J.P., and Gerbracht, G. *Teachers' Stories: From Personal Narrative to Professional Insight*. 1995, San Francisco, CA: Jossey-Bass.
19. Mintzberg, H., *Managers, Not MBAs: A Hard Look at the Soft Practice of Managing and Management Development*. 2004, San Francisco, CA: Berrett-Koehler Publishers.
20. Buckler, S.A. and Zien, K.A. The Spirituality of Innovation: Learning from Stories. *Journal of Product Innovation Management* 1996; 13(5): p. 391–405.
21. Shaw, G., Brown, R., and Bromiley, P. Strategic Stories: How 3M is Rewriting Business Planning. *Harvard Business Review* 1997; 76(3): p. 41–2, 44, 46–50.

22. Nisbett, R.E. and Ross, L. *Human Inference: Strategies and Shortcomings of Social Judgment.* 1980, Englewood Cliffs, NJ: Prentice-Hall.

23. Laufer, A. and Hoffman, E.J. *Project Management Success Stories: Lessons of Project Leaders.* 2000, New York, NY: Wiley & Sons: pp. 233–34.

24. Lee, D. Transfer Wisdom Workshops: Coming to a NASA Center Near You. *Ask Magazine* 2003; 12: p. 15–9.

25. Rodgers, T. "Trusting the Enemy." *Ask Magazine* 2003; 12: p. 18.

26. Bauschlicher, J. Get in Bed. *Ask Magazine* 2003; 12: p. 19.

7

Tailoring Project Decisions to Project Context

"One cool judgment is worth a thousand hasty councils."
Woodrow Wilson

This book highlights the shift in the focus and practices of successful project managers from the past—when the project environment was assumed to be in "geometric order"—to today's turbulent times, when the project environment exists in "living order." It is natural that when the environment is considered stable and orderly, project managers focus on repetitive and standard ways of overseeing work. But in chaotic and unpredictable environments, "uniqueness and originality ... should instead characterize the project," as Melgrati and Damiani concluded [1].

》a world dominated by living order requires moving from a one-size-fits-all paradigm to tailoring the decisions to the context of the specific situation

---

Indeed, a world dominated by living order requires moving from a one-size-fits-all paradigm to tailoring the decisions to the context of the specific situation. Such context-dependent decision making requires a great deal of judgment and is a challenging shift in mindset. But as Quinn, Mintzberg, and

© The Author(s) 2018
A. Laufer et al., *Becoming a Project Leader*,
https://doi.org/10.1007/978-3-319-66724-9_7

Table 7.1 The shifting landscape of project management

Key parameters	Yesterday	Today	In this book
Project environment	Geometric order	Living order	Chapter 1
Decision making	One best way	Tailored to the context	Throughout
Governance	Management	Management and leadership	Chapters 2, 3 and 4
Focus of practice	Processes	Results and processes	Chapter 3
Focus of organization	Systems	People and systems	Chapter 5
Learning venue	In class	On the job and in class	Chapter 6

James (1988) conclude, "judgement [is] the most critical attribute of any manager. … Most judgement calls are not simple selections between black and white, but are between subtle shades of gray" [2].

The four principles explained in this book—planning, agility, resilience, and collaboration—are grounded in theory and research, but presented through real-life stories told by successful project managers. The story approach—honed by the authors during years of research and consultation in a large variety of companies—is the only approach that can do justice to the reality of today's unsettling conditions of living order (summarized in Table 7.1). Since stories are highly context sensitive, their extensive use throughout the book should facilitate the required shift from a context-free mindset to a context-specific one. Project management is not easy. Nor is it something that can be quantified and programmed. But the wisdom of successful managers can indeed be transferred to those willing to take on the many roles and challenges of becoming a project leader.

References

1. Melgrati, A. and Damiani, M. Rethinking the Project Management Framework: New Epistemology, New Insights, in *Proceedings of PMI Research Conference.* 2002, Seattle, Washington.
2. Quinn, J.B., Mintzberg, H., and James, R.M. *The Strategy Process: Concepts, Contexts, and Cases.* 1988, Englewood Cliffs, New Jersey: Prentice Hall.

Index

© The Author(s) 2018
A. Laufer et al., *Becoming a Project Leader*,
https://doi.org/10.1007/978-3-319-66724-9